Presented to

Jeremy

By

Grandma & Grandpa

On the Occasion of

His moving to his
first real job.

Date

Feb. 26. 2000

The Word on Life

Toni Sortor
and
Pamela McQuade

BARBOUR
PUBLISHING, INC.
Uhrichsville, Ohio

Published by Barbour Publishing, Inc., P.O. Box 719, Uhrichsville, OH 44683 http://www.barbourbooks.com

Member of the
Evangelical Christian
Publishers Association

Printed in the United States of America.

Preface

You've waited a long time for this.

You're on your own, making your way through a great big world full of opportunity, adventure, and challenge.

So what's in store for you now? A job, that's for sure. It may not be the best job in the world, or even close. It might not be what you've "always wanted to do." But you have to start somewhere and begin to build a resumé that fills at least one sheet of paper.

How about a place of your own? It probably won't be a palace. In fact, it might be too small and in need of some repairs. But it will be *yours*, and soon you'll be making plans for moving into a bigger and better place.

This stage of life is exciting, but it may be a lot harder than you ever imagined. For much of your life, you've lived by other peoples' rules, and even though they were sometimes confining, at least you had some guidelines to live by. Now you have to make your own decisions. Do you spend money faster than you can earn it, snapping up all the latest clothes and electronics? Or do you develop the self-discipline needed to live within your wages and maybe even save a little? Do you spend your free time partying, or do you invest it in volunteer work or classes that will help you get ahead in your career? Do you stop going to church because your parents aren't there to wake you up on Sunday morning, or do you get up and show up on time? The decisions just keep coming.

To make good decisions, you need good information. If you're thinking of buying a particular automobile, you talk to others who own that kind of car and read the reviews in consumer magazines. If you're making a life-changing decision, or debating a point of morality, you turn to the one source of good information that will never steer you wrong: the Bible. As God's Word, you can trust it completely.

This book, *The Word on Life*, will point you to some key passages in the Bible—passages that deal with the issues you'll face as you're out on your own. This book isn't a replacement for the Bible. But perhaps it can help you through this crucial time, and point you in the right direction as you make decisions and choices, both small and large. Get ready for the adventure of your life—and read on for *The Word on Life*!

January 1

Therefore, if anyone is in Christ,
he is a new creation;
the old has gone, the new has come!
2 CORINTHIANS 5:17

New Year's often turns into an excuse for excess. There are too many relatives around the house, too much food on the table, too many football games to watch. The day rarely lives up to its promise. It turns a little flat about midafternoon, and by evening we're relieved that it's nearly over.

The thing we like about New Year's, though, is that it marks a new beginning. Maybe last year was a bummer, but now we celebrate hope for the year to come. Tomorrow we'll probably break all our resolutions, but today we allow ourselves to dream a little.

We don't have to settle for just dreams, though. As the verse above says, if you've given your life to the Lord, everything really *is* new. Your old sins are forgiven, and you're as clean as the falling snow. Anything *is* possible, with God's help. And that is really something worth celebrating!

Father, on this day of celebration and resolutions, remind me that I have good reason to hope. You will be by my side this year, helping me make my dreams come true every day.

January 2

A poor man is shunned by all his relatives—
how much more do his friends avoid him!
Though he pursues them with pleading,
they are nowhere to be found.
PROVERBS 19:7

What a sad picture! This poor guy's relatives don't want him around because he's an embarrassment to the whole family. And now his friends won't even return his calls. He doesn't understand. Sure, he's broke—but how could everyone turn on him like this?

This guy has probably become a pain in the neck. He's asked too many relatives for loans he'll never repay. He's mooched too many meals and movies from his friends. His constant cries for help have turned everyone off.

His poverty probably isn't his fault. Stuff like that just happens. But obviously his reaction to poverty has been too extreme and he has driven everyone away. He's forgotten that it's not the amount of money you have but your faith in God that's important. Some people can handle both poverty and wealth with grace; others spend all their time whining.

Father, money is scarce right now. I know things will get better for me later, but I'm a little scared. Help me survive this with good humor and hope, so those I love will never want to hide from me.

January 3

*On the first day of every week,
each one of you should set aside
a sum of money in keeping with his income,
saving it up. . .*
1 CORINTHIANS 16:2

I n the old days, budgeting was simple. You bought a flat metal lockbox with compartments. Then you physically divided up your salary, putting one quarter of your monthly expenses in each compartment. Of course, some expenses didn't fit any category, and at least one compartment usually came up short at the end of the month. But the system gave you some self-control.

You can set up a system like this on a computer, so your bank account doesn't leak like a sieve. The important part—and the least fun—is sitting down with a calculator to figure out exactly how much money has to go in each compartment each month. A budgeting book from the library can help. It's not a perfect system. But it will tell you how long it will be before you can lease that car.

Father, I need to get a handle on my money. I need to know where it's all going and what I'm doing wrong. Give me the patience to sit down and do this budgeting—and then give me the self-control I need to make it work.

January 4

*It is not good to have
zeal without knowledge,
nor to be hasty and miss the way.*
PROVERBS 19:2

You've got dreams and goals and energy to spare. Like a cat locked out of a bedroom, you want to throw yourself against all obstacles. Well, the cat never gets on the bed that way. It doesn't know how to turn the doorknob, after all.

But one night the cat tries another approach. He cries—pitifully, loudly, for minutes on end—and because you love him, *you* open the door and let him hog the bed. The cat has achieved his goal, hasn't he? He may never learn how to turn a doorknob, but he figured out a way around that problem.

Sometimes, like the cat, you just have to step back and think a problem through. Hitting your head against a door may not do the trick.

Father, I know what I want out of life, and I'm determined to achieve my goals with Your help. Give me the sense to figure out how to do this with the least possible amount of pain, and if my goals are not pleasing to You, put me on the right track.

January 5

*The fear of the LORD is
the beginning of wisdom:
a good understanding have all they
that do his commandments.*
PSALM 111:10, KJV

We all need to feel we are respected. Unfortunately, respect is hard to earn when you're young. If you haven't been with a company for a few years, almost no one will bother to listen to your good ideas, let alone act on them. Some supervisors will even steal your ideas, taking the credit that rightfully belongs to you! What should you do?

Two paths lead to respect, and the one you choose determines your future—so choose carefully. The first path comes most naturally. You watch your back, strike before you're struck, and butter up the right people until you've clawed yourself to the top.

What's the second path? Follow the principles laid down by the Lord. This is not the easy way. It's not a shortcut, and at times it doesn't even seem to work. But it will soon give you self-respect—the first step on the path to success.

Father, help me choose wisely when I come to life's crossroads. Give me wisdom to choose the Lamb's path, not the tiger's. Help me be someone who is respected for the way I live, not for the damage I can do.

January 6

Now no chastening for the present seemeth to be joyous, but grievous: nevertheless afterward it yieldeth the peaceable fruit of righteousness unto them which are exercised thereby.
HEBREWS 12:11, KJV

It's a good idea to understand the distinction between office culture and office politics. The two are often hard to separate. Suppose, for instance, every man in your building wears a tie and jacket, even if they take the jacket off when they get down to work. Every woman wears dress pants or a skirt with a jacket. If you're a man, you may be tempted to buy one tie and skip the jacket; if you're a woman, you may think you can get by with jeans and a blazer. Eventually, though, someone is going to comment on your clothes. No matter how brilliant you are, when you buck office culture, you are not showing proper respect. People will notice.

Office culture is not the same as office politics. Office culture is a form of discipline that dictates how things will get done. It's an organizing force that leads to productivity.

Before you decide to rebel, make sure what it is you're fighting—office politics or office culture.

Lord, teach me to choose my battles carefully. Give me insight into my job's culture.

January 7

The Lord is not slow in keeping his promise, as some understand slowness. He is patient with you, not wanting anyone to perish, but everyone to come to repentance.
2 PETER 3:9

A week has passed since you made your New Year's resolutions. How many of them are you still keeping? Well, we're all human. Promises come easily to us and are just as easily forgotten.

Of all the promises we make and break, perhaps the most tragic are those we make to God. "Get me out of this and I promise. . ." Every time we say something like that, in the back of our minds we can hear God say, "Oh, sure!" And yet we keep promising, for who else can we turn to in times of real crisis?

Isn't it wonderful to know "He is patient with you, not wanting anyone to perish"? As often as we make and break our little promises, God never breaks a one. Once His word is given, it's forever.

Father, help me be more faithful at keeping my word. My track record is pretty bad, but I look to You and Your promises as examples to follow.

January 8

For thou art my lamp, O LORD:
and the LORD will lighten my darkness.
2 SAMUEL 22:29, KJV

The holidays are over. All that looms ahead is winter, going to work in the dark, and coming home in the dark. Winter can be lonely and depressing.

It's time to make some new friends. Easier said than done, of course. The bar scene's not for you. But just because you're a Christian, you don't have to hide away from humanity. The light of your faith can't shine in the world if you never get out into it.

Start with baby steps. Get out of the apartment. Do something—anything—that will let you hear human voices and interact with others. Next step: Volunteer. Forget about yourself and really become engaged in something outside yourself. Third step: Invite someone over. Host a Bible study that needs a home. Your apartment's big enough, no matter how small it is.

Soon your phone will be ringing, your weekends full, and you'll see the buds of developing friendships. You and the Lord will have turned your darkness into light.

Lord, I have much to offer others and am willing to work at sharing what I have. Help me keep my mind off my own darkness and focused on brightening the lives of others.

January 9

Do not forsake your friend.
PROVERBS 27:10

One of the saddest days in your life could be the one when you realize things will never be the same again between you and your old friends. You've moved away from the old neighborhood and so have most of your friends. Besides, you are working different hours, dating, married, have new interests.

Fight it! Call the parents of your old friends, get phone numbers, then use them. Every time you're in town, look somebody up. Organize a weekend get-together.

Sometimes you'll strike out. A few of the group will drop out of your life totally. Others will have changed so much that you have nothing in common anymore. But a few will respond, and if you keep in touch, keep interested in each other, and spend the necessary time, you will develop new and more mature relationships. It won't be the same as before, but the friendships you cherish can survive. All it takes is one determined person who refuses to let the good times be forgotten.

Lord, I know that growth means change, but some things are too good to let die. Help me be the one who keeps us all in touch when life tries to keep us apart.

January 10

*But since there is so much immorality,
each man should have his own wife,
and each woman her own husband.*
1 CORINTHIANS 7:2

Sounds like what your mother's been saying ever since you graduated, doesn't it? Some of your friends are happily married, a lot are determined to stay single until their biological clock approaches midnight, others are in marriages that are coming apart at the seams. You have friends who never stop trying to fix you up and others who applaud your singleness. Who's right?

You are! If you're single, that's what's right for you right now. You'll get all kinds of advice from everyone who cares for you, but never allow yourself to be pressured, either way. Marriage is an event of the heart, not a calculated decision.

When it's time for you to marry, you'll know. Suddenly, you'll want to see this one face across the breakfast table every day of your life. Marriage will no longer seem a threat but a promise.

Father, I want to be loved, but I'm not sure I want to be married. Give me confidence in my own feelings and make whatever I decide right for me, in line with Your design for my life.

January 11

*When God gives any man
wealth and possessions,
and enables him to enjoy them,
to accept his lot and be happy in his work—
this is a gift of God.*
ECCLESIASTES 5:19

Your parents probably have no more spare cash than you do. After all, your living expenses are less than theirs at this point, and they're trying to save up for retirement. Your father may have been downsized a few times, your brothers and sisters have taken their share for educational expenses, and pension plans aren't what they used to be.

That doesn't mean you can't go to your parents for help if you can't pay your rent or put food on the table. You may even have to move back in with them. But if you are making a decent wage, you need to pay your own way—and cut your expenses if you aren't.

There's no need to pity your parents or suffer from guilt when you need help. They consider you a good investment, and you haven't disappointed them. You are their gift from God—and their gift to God.

Lord, I'm not sure how financially secure my parents are these days, but I need to be independent now, for everyone's sake, and learn to handle my own money wisely.

January 12

Let no man despise thy youth;
but be thou an example of the believers,
in word, in conversation, in charity,
in spirit, in faith, in purity.
1 TIMOTHY 4:12, KJV

When someone's referred to as a "good example," most likely that person is middle-aged or older. We tend to look to those who are older than we are for inspiration, figuring they have more experience and wisdom. That is not necessarily true; there are plenty of old fools around.

Don't rule yourself out of the good example population because you're young. Being a good example has nothing to do with age and everything to do with how you live your life. You can be a good example in kindergarten, providing you don't run with scissors.

You don't have to be a Goody Two-shoes, but you should try to live your life with courage and fairness and faith. If you can do that long enough, you're on your way toward becoming a good example. A good reputation opens doors that might otherwise stay closed to you.

Lord, I'm not sure I want to be a good example. Maybe for now I'll just concentrate on doing the right thing day by day and see how it works out. Teach me how I should act.

January 13

Dear brothers and sisters, don't be childish in your understanding of these things. Be innocent as babies when it comes to evil, but be mature and wise in understanding matters of this kind.
1 CORINTHIANS 14:20, NLT

Children do not come into the world with morals. They know nothing about good and evil when they're born. Good and evil mean nothing to toddlers until their parents teach them the difference.

Our culture likes to pretend that evil doesn't exist today—that anything you want to do is okay or that an evil person was somehow made that way by circumstances. In effect, society is saying that it's okay to think like a child.

It's a bunch of baloney. Most individuals brought up in bad circumstances turn out to be good people because they were *taught* to be good people. They were held responsible for their actions as children and continue to act responsibly.

Maybe parts of our culture think it's okay to act like a child forever, to give in to every whim and not care how your behavior affects others, but that's childish thinking. Your mother taught you better than that!

Father, keep me aware of the difference between good and evil and help me be a responsible adult. Society may believe that anything goes, but I know better.

January 14

How can a young man keep his way pure?
By living according to your word.
PSALM 119:9

Finding time to read is hard—but why not dig your copy of the Bible out and put it where you'll see it every day? It has everything you need in it. It has plenty of action and suspense, not to mention memorable characters. If you run into something you don't understand, you can flip the page and find a new subject. If you're dealing with a problem in your life, the answers to it are in the Bible. Plus it can be read in short spurts. You can read a whole psalm while the bread is toasting.

Most important, the Bible will teach you how to live according to God's wishes. You can't be a good person without knowing what a good person does. Invest in a concordance and you'll be able to find everything the Bible says about whatever subject interests you. Then you'll know what God wants you to do. Life *does* come with an instruction book.

Father, when I have a question about what I should do in a certain circumstance, remind me that all Your answers are there for me in Your Word.

January 15

*Always be prepared to give an answer
to everyone who asks you to give
the reason for the hope that you have.
But do this with gentleness and respect.*
1 PETER 3:15

Christians should be rich in hope, secure in the blessings they see ahead. Even when times are tough, they have faith in the future.

This confuses people. "You just lost your job? How can you smile?" "Your car's been totaled? How can you be so calm?" When people have known you for a while and seen that you *consistently* react with hope, they will be impressed and truly want to know how you do it.

You don't have to give a long theological answer. Be gentle. Since you probably already know these people, you can tailor your answer so that you show respect for their beliefs.

You've sat around and participated in bull sessions about politics, life on other planets, and the perfect mate. The rules are the same here. Don't let the word *witnessing* scare you when people seem truly interested in gaining a little hope for themselves.

Father, give me wisdom when people ask me about my faith. Help me answer their questions with gentleness and respect, bringing glory to You.

January 16

But let every man prove his own work,
and then shall he have rejoicing in himself alone,
and not in another.
For every man shall bear his own burden.
GALATIANS 6:4–5, KJV

Once you graduate and go out into the world, peer pressure lessens, although you will always have some pressure from the groups to which you belong —work groups, church groups, social groups, and so on. At this point in life, though, you have more groups from which to choose, and their demands are more moderate, so you have more freedom. You have the chance to "reinvent" yourself. A shy high school student can choose to speak out in a new group. A follower can become a leader, or a leader can decide to take a break.

Now is the time to become the person you've always thought you could be. Carefully choose the groups with whom you want to associate. Assume responsibility for your own actions and take pride in the way you live, "for each one should carry his own load" (v. 5 NIV).

Lord, now that I have the freedom to be whoever I want to be, help me make wise choices. I want to live a life I can be proud of, and I know You have something special in mind for me.

January 17

*Serve wholeheartedly,
as if you were serving the Lord, not men.*
EPHESIANS 6:7

Young people are noted for their vitality and enthusiasm. God likes that attitude so much that He promises to reward those who show that kind of wholeheartedness in their work, doing it as if they were working for Him instead of for their bosses.

Unfortunately, age and experience seem to take the edge off our enthusiasm. Some jobs just don't reward it. At first, employers welcome enthusiasm, but then it begins to annoy them. Like too much sugar, enthusiasm can become—well, just *too much.*

How do you strike a good balance? Look at someone older than yourself, someone well respected and successful at work, and see how that person operates. You'll see she's thorough in her work, quiet and humble, but when she speaks, people listen. They know in her own quiet way, she's working wholeheartedly.

She probably started off just like you, but she was able to rein herself in until she learned her job. If you, too, can learn to harness your energy productively, you'll be on your way to success.

Father, show me how to channel my enthusiasm into solid work that pleases both my employer and You.

January 18

There's nothing wrong with making plans—but ultimately, all our plans depend upon the will of God, and sometimes His will and ours are not the same. He knows when our plans won't get us where we should be, so sometimes He puts a roadblock in front of our carefully thought-out path and nudges us in another direction—while we mutter and complain about the detour.

This doesn't mean we shouldn't plan at all and leave everything to God. That would be aimlessly wandering around without purpose. We have to be flexible in our planning, though, aware that several roads may lead us where we want to be. We may not be able to see far enough ahead to plan the route, but God can, and His plans for us will never fail.

Lord, be patient with all my plans and dreams, even the ones You know won't work out the way I think they will. You've given me this need to look ahead, so it must be a good thing. Now give me the faith to trust You when everything falls apart, knowing You will lead me onto the right path for my life.

January 19

Let us purify ourselves from everything
that contaminates body and spirit,
perfecting holiness out of reverence for God.
2 CORINTHIANS 7:1

U nless you plan to live the life of a hermit, this verse is going to give you problems. We live in a thoroughly contaminated world where it's difficult to be even a little holy, let alone perfectly holy.

Start with the most important fact, though: Your sins have *already* been forgiven. How do you thank someone for saving your life now and forever? By trying to be what He wants you to be. No, you are not going to do it perfectly. Yes, you will still sin. But you will steer clear of situations that God disapproves of. You will treat your body as the holy temple of God, who lives in you. You will treat others the way you want to be treated. It's a start, anyway, and this is one case where good intentions *do* count.

Father, I can never live my life in total holiness, but I can show my thankfulness and reverence for You in many ways. Help me live my life in a way that will reflect Your glory and mercy and eternal love.

January 20

*Let your conversation be without covetousness;
and be content with such things as ye have:
for he hath said, I will never leave thee,
nor forsake thee.*
HEBREWS 13:5, KJV

Love of money is not handling well what you have, investing and providing for your future. It's not even buying some things for fun. All these are perfectly valid uses of money. God wants you to prosper and enjoy your success.

But He wants you to keep money in perspective. Money is good, but other things are better. Wouldn't you give everything you have to pay the bill if your sister or brother needed a lifesaving operation? If a disaster made you abandon your apartment, would you save your checkbook or your roommate?

Those are pretty extreme examples, but you get the point. An excessive love of money can put your soul in danger. It can shatter marriages, turn family members against one another, and turn you into someone you'd never choose for a friend. Think about it the next time you deposit your paycheck.

Lord, I know You will provide for me. Keep me from the love of money. I want to be someone of whom You can be proud.

January 21

*But among you there must not be
even a hint of sexual immorality,
or of any kind of impurity, or of greed,
because these are improper for
God's holy people.*
EPHESIANS 5:3

Once you declare your Christianity, your life is under a microscope. If you slip, all your nice words are useless.

You can't shrug this problem off by saying it's not *you* people should follow, but Christ, who was without sin. You are the one who makes Christ visible to the world. If you intend to be an evangelist, you'd better have your own life in order.

Does this mean you can't witness to anyone because your own life is flawed? Of course not. It does mean you have to voluntarily acknowledge your own shortcomings, admitting you are a flawed mirror of God; your own sins come between others and the glory you're trying to reflect. When you admit that, people can see you as honest, a normal human being, then look beyond you and glimpse the possibility of their own salvation.

Father, I'm not worthy to be an example of You and Your way of life. Help me deal with my own sins in a way that will bring glory to You and salvation to other sinners like me.

January 22

*A righteous man cares for
the needs of his animal.*
PROVERBS 12:10

Living on your own is lonely. Eventually, you may start thinking about a dog, especially if you grew up with one. How nice it would be to open the door and have a puppy run into your arms! He'd curl up beside you in bed, protect the apartment while you're gone, and shower you with love.

But can you care for the needs of a dog? What would you do with him when you're at work? Let him tear up the apartment in frustration? Keep him in a cage? Your needs are important, but what would the dog get out of such a relationship, besides hours of loneliness? And what happens when you move, which most young people do often? Can you find a new apartment where dogs are allowed?

Righteous people take responsibility for the well-being of every animal they bring into their lives. Before you adopt that puppy, be sure you are ready for a fifteen-year commitment.

Father, I know it's not fair to use others, even a pet, to enrich my own life at their expense. Help me see this before I bring home a pet I can't care for properly.

January 23

There are "friends" who destroy each other,
but a real friend sticks closer than a brother.
PROVERBS 18:24, NLT

Companions are easier to find than friends. They can be a little wacky, a little wild, a little irresponsible—but you certainly wouldn't want to introduce them to your mother when she comes to visit.

Companions come and go rapidly. They wear out their welcome or decide you've worn out yours, and it's no big deal when you part ways, since no one has any emotional commitment. You've had a few good times, that's all.

Of course you can't depend on companions for anything. If they're in the mood they might help you move—once. They may lend you a twenty—once. But when you really need them, they'll be busy.

Fortunately, a few companions become friends. They hang around longer than usual. You find you have several interests in common and begin to talk seriously about deeper, more personal things. If you're really in tune with each other, you invest in each other, although you'd never say something like that. You'll just be there.

We all need friends like this.

Father, help me be careful in my choice of companions and willing to be a good friend.

January 24

*And he said, "Verily, I say unto you,
No prophet is accepted in his own country."*
LUKE 4:24, KJV

Jesus knew what many young people have learned through experience: If you want to get ahead in life, you may have to leave your hometown.

Why does it seem easier to get ahead elsewhere? For one thing, everyone knows you too well in your hometown. Even if they remember good things about you, you are still a little boy or girl in their minds, not a competent mechanic or stock market broker.

But not everyone can or wants to leave home. They work diligently, invest their time and money in their hometowns, and grow in the eyes of their old neighbors until they become town elders themselves. It takes a while, but the rewards are great, because hometowners love those who do well right where they were planted.

Whether you stay or go is an extremely personal decision. No one knows what you want as well as you do. Ask the Lord to give you guidance, then follow your heart. Besides, this is not an unchangeable decision—you *can* go home again.

Father, You know what I value most in life. Help me sort out my priorities and do what's right for me.

January 25

Anyone who claims to be in the light but hates his brother is still in the darkness. Whoever loves his brother lives in the light.
1 JOHN 2:9–10

Although this verse is talking about loving our brothers and sisters in a universal way, it also applies to actual family members, because if you can't love your actual brother, how can you say you love everyone?

Brothers and sisters come with a lot of emotional baggage. For twenty years you've disliked your brother or looked up to him, considered him a bum or admired him. Sometimes you've loved your sister, sometimes you've hated her. Sometimes you fought with her, sometimes you fought for her.

Maybe your brothers and sisters are your best friends—maybe they're not. Either way, if you're a Christian, you must still love all your brothers and sisters in general, and that includes your brothers and sisters in blood. If you claim to love everyone, you can't exclude anyone. Why would you want to? They're your family.

Father, it's easy to say I love everyone, but sometimes I don't even treat my actual brothers and sisters with love. Give me patience and understanding for everyone, including those in my family.

January 26

When you're intoxicatingly in love, you always promise more than you can deliver. Let's be clear on one point, though: This type of promise is not the same as the promises we make when we marry. Those are not to be broken, under any circumstances. We're talking about impossible promises, such as "I promise I won't even *look* at another man for as long as I live." "I want you by my side every day of my life," you say, forgetting to add "except during football season."

We go on making promises like this because no one is totally sane when they are in love. As human beings, our love will always be as imperfect as we are. But with God's help, we can be faithful to the promises that count.

Father, help the one I love to be patient with me when I goof up—and help me stay true to the promises that can absolutely never be broken.

January 27

Houses and wealth are inherited from parents,
but a prudent wife is from the LORD.
PROVERBS 19:14

Being prudent doesn't mean being cheap. It does mean being careful and thrifty. Some people are brought up to be savers, though, while others are spenders. A saver who falls into sudden money will still be a saver. A spender who goes bust will still spend whatever he has.

A couple that is mismatched in their financial philosophy is headed for trouble. This isn't something we usually think about when we fall in love and contemplate marriage, but it should be. After dating someone for months, you should have some idea of how he or she handles money. You're not looking for a perfect match. A person who is a little too cheap might do well to marry one who spends a little more freely, and vice versa. What you need is a person more or less like you, different within tolerable limits. Then at least you will be on the same wavelength when you discuss money issues.

In the end, you and your spouse will decide what is prudent, given your circumstances, so be sure you agree about your priorities.

Lord, help me spend my money wisely, and give me a mate who shares my thoughts on this subject so we don't fall into the trap of arguing about money and its uses.

January 28

Let every soul be subject unto the higher powers.
For there is no power but of God:
the powers that be are ordained of God.
ROMANS 13:1, KJV

God knows we need rules and regulations in society, or all would be chaos. The problem comes when we confuse our rulers with the governing system itself. We hate paying taxes, but we can't abolish the Internal Revenue Service and watch the government default on its obligations. No one likes to get a speeding ticket, but what would the roads be like without speed limits and people to enforce them?

As someone once said, the United States has a peaceful revolution every four years. If you are upset about the acts of a government official, get out there and vote.

God doesn't go into detail about governing authorities. He wants us to obey the laws we have created, but other than that, He left it up to us to form our own government. We're all part of "the system," and we all must obey its regulations—or change them in a peaceful manner.

Father, I know we have a human government, so it will always have problems. Give me faith in what we have created over the years and the courage to work toward peacefully changing what I don't like.

January 29

You learned a lot from your parents, mostly through example. You learned that Sunday feels empty without church. You learned that sharing often gets you twice as much as hogging. You learned that hitting causes more problems than talking and disrespect is often worse than hitting. You absorbed all these lessons and more through your day-to-day life at home.

At the same time, you were learning at school and on the playground. Some of these lessons were harsh, but they were also useful. You had to know what the world was really like.

You often laughed when your parents told you, "We don't do things like that in this family," but the next time it came up in the world, you didn't do it. It didn't feel right.

The older you get, the more you will remember your parents' lessons, and the more thankful you will be. Soon enough, you'll be telling your own children, "We don't do that in *this* family!"

Father, I hope I'll be able to teach my children as well as my parents taught me. Their lessons always came out of their love for me. I'll do my best to pass them on.

January 30

*A man who lacks judgment
derides his neighbor,
but a man of understanding
holds his tongue.*
PROVERBS 11:12

In a very real way, you made your neighbors the way they are. Most neighbors start out as neutral. They're willing to give you a chance because a good neighborhood is profitable to them, both emotionally and financially. If you go out of your way to be pleasant, so will they. If you're inconsiderate and rude, that's exactly what you'll get back.

So you're out on your own now, free for the first time to live as you please and play your music as loud as you want. You can party until dawn in your own apartment and let the garbage pile up as long as you want.

At first, the comments will be mild. "Good party, I heard." "Could you keep the music down a little?" "Did some animal die in there?" An apology and a slight mending of your ways can fix it all right away, but if you react with hostility, the police will be uninvited guests at your next party.

What exactly do you want your neighbor to be like? It's really up to you.

Father, teach me the rules of being a good neighbor. Remind me my neighbors have rights, too.

January 31

Or better a meal at Wendy's with a friend than a sirloin with the boss. One's going to be a lot more fun, that's for sure. Unfortunately, on the way up the ladder, you're going to have to eat that sirloin.

It's nice to be able to relax and enjoy your meal with friends your own age. Maybe you're all broke, but a pot of pasta tastes great in good company. You can laugh and joke without worrying about offending anyone or exhibiting your less than perfect manners.

This type of meal will be much more common than business meals. But soon you'll be able to handle yourself properly at both functions. Remember, God is present at every meal you eat, no matter who you're with—and He can use you to His glory whether you're at Wendy's with your friends or at a formal dinner party with the boss.

Father, it's nice to be invited to these business functions, but it's sure not my idea of fun. Help me learn how to act properly when I have to, out of respect for those who are generous enough to invite me.

February 1

And Jacob loved Rachel; and said,
"I will serve thee seven years for Rachel
thy younger daughter."
GENESIS 29:18, KJV

Such a storybook romance! Jacob loved Rachel so much that even seven years of service weren't too much. How could a woman resist such a man?

When you start dating seriously and things look good, stars light up your eyes. Your date seems perfect, and almost nothing would keep you apart. Bad weather and inconvenient schedules can't separate you.

But time has a way of changing that glow. Seven weeks (or seven months) later, when you know your date's faults better, you may wonder how Jacob held out so long. With your dating partner, you decide, he never would have made it!

Relationships weren't made to be worn like favorite T-shirts that are thrown away when they get ratty. Instead of picking on each other, prayerfully sit down and try to iron out your troubles. After all, Jacob and Rachel didn't have a trouble-free life, but they shared lifelong love.

As Valentine's Day approaches, are you looking for hearts and flowers or a love that lasts?

Lord, I don't want to toss away relationships like old clothes. If I need to, help me work them out.

February 2

Do not deceive yourselves.
If any one of you thinks he is wise by
the standards of this age, he should become
a "fool" so that he may become wise.
1 CORINTHIANS 3:18

Why don't you guys just leave me alone! Punxsutawney Phil probably thinks today, as those strange humans drag him out of his nice, cozy hole. *You fools! Ask a* weatherman *about spring. I just want more sleep.*

From all the groundhog hoopla, you'd think a lot of silly humans take a rodent's "prediction" about how long winter will last seriously!

Spiritually, people can be pretty ridiculous, too. Like the nonbelievers who see Christians as fools for believing they can really know God.

These people ignore God, but *you're* the fool. *Right?*

But what does the world know about wisdom? Can your boss understand a worker's deep-hearted needs? Can your non-Christian friends explain how the universe got here?

God can.

Why accept what a fool says is wise? Go instead with wisdom's Creator!

Lord, I feel uncomfortable calling people fools. But that's what You call those who reject Your love. Help me reach out to them today.

February 3

I felt I had to write and urge you to contend for the faith that was once for all entrusted to the saints.

JUDE 3

Feel as if no one ever trusts you?

God does.

Not only did He bring you to faith in Him, He entrusted you with the important task of passing it on to others, too.

If Christians never shared the faith, where would the Good News be? Should all Christians stop witnessing, destroy their Bibles, and disobediently ignore the trust God has given them, in a short time the world would be even worse than it is today. How many people would know what God has said?

During the early Middle Ages, Irish monks on the island of Iona carefully copied the Scriptures. While continental Europe was torn by political unrest and few people could pass on the Word, they painstakingly copied it letter by letter, keeping it alive. Because of their faithful efforts, we have the testimony of God's Word today.

Who needs to see or hear the gospel your life can pass on today?

Lord, I want to share Your Good News today. Show me someone who needs to hear it.

February 4

I am not writing you a new command but one we have had from the beginning. I ask that we love one another. And this is love: that we walk in obedience to his commands.

2 JOHN 5–6

Sometimes being a Christian gets confusing. Pressures bear down, and your love grows cold. Spiritual winter sets in. So you start looking for something you've missed, some new trick to alter your life.

The truth is, you probably don't need a trick. You just need to get a handle on the old truth that's stared you in the face for a long time. Then you need to obey what you know.

When your love for God grows cold, take a fresh look at what He's already said. Draw close to the fire of His Word, and your life will alight.

When the cold, dull days of winter make you feel dull, too, renew your love for God. Warm yourself at the Scripture just as you'd seek the heat of a fireplace.

Jesus, I already know so much about You, but sometimes I don't use that knowledge in my life. Help me bridge the gap between my head and heart.

February 5

*Dear friend, you are faithful in
what you are doing for the brothers,
even though they are strangers to you.*
3 JOHN 5

We don't mind having friends visit. We'll pull out the best towels and make sure enough groceries fill the refrigerator. But when a missionary or evangelist—or worse than that, our least-favorite relative—needs a place to stay, are we "too busy"?

Gaius, an elder in a young Asian church, had plenty of demands on his time. But that didn't stop him from warmly welcoming the missionaries who crossed his path. Because he did such a great job, someone told the apostle John about it.

Gaius probably shared the doubts we have about entertaining guests. Would they make a mess of the house? Eat him out of house and home? Be so irritating that after a day he'd want to toss them out in the street? But he invited them in anyway.

Even if your cousin Poindexter messes up your bathroom, you can clean it again once he's gone. But you can't clean up your own heart if you sinned by ignoring God's commands for hospitality.

Giving up some of my space is hard, Lord. But I want to use my home to show Your love. Open my heart to help.

February 6

Will a man rob God? Yet you rob me.
But you ask, "How do we rob you?"
In tithes and offerings. You are under a curse—
the whole nation of you—
because you are robbing me.
MALACHI 3:8–9

Billions of dollars are spent in America every year on R-rated movies. Each weekend, people throng to the latest violent blockbuster and plunk down their cash for entertainment.

Meanwhile, the view in other areas of America is hardly "entertaining." Churches can barely stay above water financially because so few people tithe, and some needy families only get help when their story reaches the six o'clock news.

Is it any surprise our nation is in trouble?

If we gave as generously to God as we do to our entertainment, imagine the people who could be helped. Churches could expand ministries to the inner city and support ministries all over the world. There'd be enough money to help a family get back on its feet following the breadwinner's illness.

God promises a curse to the nation that cheats Him, but the blessings that come with generous giving can hardly be imagined.

Let's start the blessing today.

Lord, entertainment isn't anything compared to You. Help me give to You first, not last.

February 7

Who am I, O Lord GOD? and what is my house,
that thou hast brought me hitherto?
2 SAMUEL 7:18, KJV

Who prayed this incredibly humble prayer?

Israel's greatest king, the man after God's own heart—David!

By the end of his life, David, who had received so much from God, knew better than to "obey" God on his own terms. God had told the king that his son, Solomon, would build the temple, and even though David cherished this service for God, he humbly accepted God's decree.

After all, God had taken the shepherd boy and made him a king—he could also take the king and make him a shepherd again. David understood that without God he was nothing.

When everything's going fine spiritually, you may want to do a great work for God and start planning it. Though you can't imagine why, suddenly it falls apart.

Do you go back where you should have started—prayer and obedience—or do you forge on, figuring it will all work out later?

Who do you think you are—a shepherd boy or a king?

Heavenly Father, when I want to serve You, I need to be humble. Tune my heart to Yours, and let me never jump ahead of Your plans.

February 8

Joash said to the priests, "Collect all the money that is brought as sacred offerings. . . . And let it be used to repair whatever damage is found in the temple."
2 KINGS 12:4–5

J oash, a good king in a long line of bad kings of Judah, certainly had the best of intentions when he collected money to repair the temple. But twenty-three years later, the project remained at a standstill.

Well-meaning Joash lacked follow-through. Why would it take so long for him to notice that the carpenters and stonemasons hadn't done their work? Didn't the king visit the temple weekly?

Whether we're talking about a king or ordinary Christian, just pouring money into a project isn't enough. It's not only important to collect money for missions, you have to send the money to the missionaries, follow up on how it's been used, pray for them, keep in touch, and invite them to visit and share with the church the next time they're in the area.

Like Joash, we can't remember God one day and then let Him sit, unnoticed, for years.

It's easy to get excited about Your Kingdom, Lord, when an idea is new, but I want to be steady. Teach me to finish the things I start for You.

February 9

*Beware lest any man spoil you
through philosophy and vain deceit,
after the tradition of men, after the rudiments
of the world, and not after Christ.*
COLOSSIANS 2:8, KJV

We expect the world to try to disagree with us. After all, those who don't know Jesus aren't going to believe everything we do.

But what happens when people in our churches face us with ideas that aren't biblical or philosophies that owe less to Christianity than something else?

It's nothing new. God hasn't forgotten His church. The Colossians had the same problem.

People in this New Testament church fought off heresy from within. No longer were the apostles' teachings and the Hebrew Scriptures enough. Among other things, the heretics taught the need for a secret knowledge and angel worship. They said you needed "something more" than Jesus.

If someone comes along teaching something "new" or different about Jesus, don't listen. God hasn't hidden anything you need to know about Jesus—it's all in His Book.

Anything else has no authority at all.

Jesus, I don't need anything "new" about You. I just need to know You better and better. Draw me close to You through Your Word.

February 10

These are the words of the Son of God. . . .
"I know your deeds, your love and faith,
your service and perseverance,
and that you are now doing more
than you did at first."
REVELATION 2:18–19

If I'd known what I was getting into," Rita exclaimed to her pastor, "I never would have become Danielle's friend. I tried to help her out of her troubles, and all she can do is complain!"

Maybe you, too, have done a good turn—you gave someone a ride, only to have her constantly call whenever she wanted to go to the store, or you gave him advice that backfired. You did good with the best intentions, but now you wish you'd never done it.

When your good deeds seem to haunt you, know that God sees beyond the situation into your heart. He knows you desired only good. He'll bless you for that desire.

Though you experienced bad side effects from your good deeds, never again helping anyone isn't an option. Turn to the One who knows your deeds and do another good deed—chances are it *won't* backfire.

Lord, I know every good deed doesn't fall apart. Help me to reach out to others, even when things don't go the way I'd like.

February 11

*For unto me the children of Israel are servants;
they are my servants whom I brought forth
out of the land of Egypt.*
LEVITICUS 25:55, KJV

Freedom from slavery. Who'd give it up?

God had set His people free when they came out of Egypt—they were only His servants, not an Egyptian's. But when life became financially desperate, some Israelites sold themselves back into slavery to other Israelites. Perhaps the harvest had been bad for years on end, and a farmer saw no other way to pay his debts.

But even selling himself as a slave didn't mean he'd be one for the rest of his life. Every fifty years, God called for the Year of Jubilee. During this liberty celebration, Hebrew slaves became free again. If he'd sold his land, he got that back, too.

Even Israelite slaves were God's servants first and foremost. God had set them free, and no one could hold on to them forever—that was His right.

If you know Jesus, God has liberated you, too. Nothing—no sin or trouble or situation—can claim you forever.

You're free!

Jesus, thank You for making me free. I want to be Your servant first and foremost.

February 12

*Miriam and Aaron began
to talk against Moses. . . .
"Has the Lord spoken only through Moses?"
they asked. "Hasn't he also spoken through us?"*
NUMBERS 12:1–2

Moses was doing a great work. He'd brought the Israelites out of Egypt, and they were nearing Canaan.

Suddenly, from within his own camp, his own family, opposition struck. Sibling jealousy attacked as Miriam and Aaron craved fame.

Within a family, jealousy's nasty. But have you seen the worse damage it creates in a church? If a young adult leader draws a crowd of people and the pastor becomes jealous, it can ruin a church. If elders play a game of one-upmanship instead of developing servanthood, it can tear the congregation apart.

You can't always keep others from being jealous of you, but you can control your own feelings. If people in your church are doing a good work, commend them, don't criticize.

God's blessed them, so be glad.

Lord, I don't want to be jealous when You're bringing people to You through someone else. Help me encourage a brother or sister for doing Your will.

February 13

*Ho, every one that thirsteth, come ye
to the waters, and he that hath no money;
come ye, buy, and eat; yea, come, buy wine
and milk without money and without price.
Wherefore do ye spend money for that which
is not bread? and your labour
for that which satisfieth not?*
ISAIAH 55:1–2, KJV

Payday!" Jim shouted to his roommate. "Can't wait to get that CD player! I'll stop at the store on my way home—and oh, baby, will it blast tonight! Maybe I'd better pick up a couple of CDs, too."

Problem was, Jim didn't have the money to buy the equipment. He got into debt with the store, which charged him an exorbitant interest rate. Already the apartment stretched Jim's budget, but it didn't seem to matter. When he was short on cash, Jim just played the music louder.

One day Jim couldn't pay the rent, and his roommate got on his case. That night the CD player blared with a new CD.

But a new CD player, new CDs, and all the noise in the world couldn't make Jim happy. Things never solve problems, because they can't fill inner emptiness or bring lasting joy. The high from a buy only lasts a short time.

Invest instead in the joy bringer—Jesus.

Lord, You know the things I need. Don't let me become a spendaholic when only You can satisfy.

February 14

Yet I hold this against you:
You have forsaken your first love.
REVELATION 2:4

Remember your first romance that gave you a glimpse of what real romantic love could be? Though it probably didn't work out, your first love sticks firmly in your mind. There was something memorable about it.

That first love probably wasn't any more exciting than the first moment you knew—really knew —that you loved Jesus. Whether you heard bells ring or just felt a quiet assurance, deep love flooded your soul. But has that first love for God turned to neglect?

If you don't spend time with your date or seek to please that special person, your relationship will show it. You'll have more disagreements than fun times. It's the same with Jesus. Though He'll love you no matter what, He won't be the overwhelming passion in your life—He'll slip into second place— or maybe third.

Has your first exciting love for God flagged, falling behind football games, the influence of a friend, your dating life, or even pizza? Ask His forgiveness and give Him every bit of your life. There's nothing better than loving Jesus.

Jesus, I don't want anyone or anything else to displace You. Be the overwhelming passion in my life.

February 15

For God hath concluded them all in unbelief,
that he might have mercy upon all.
ROMANS 11:32, KJV

Are you *glad* that Adam sinned?

Well, in a strange way, maybe you *should* be, because if all humanity hadn't sinned, none of us would really know the Father's great mercy.

Our sin *is* awful. We shouldn't wish separation from God on anyone. Because of sin, we lead complex, messy lives.

Most of us would prefer not to get involved when a friend's own choices have landed her in nasty, ongoing problems—especially when those situations are likely to impact our lives, too. Could we blame God for wanting to ignore these difficulties we brought on ourselves?

But God, in His immeasurable mercy, didn't flinch from becoming involved in our grubby lives. Instead, even before we'd sinned, He'd designed a plan to straighten us out.

Seeing such mercy reaches deep down in our souls, changing them forever. Suddenly we, too, can get involved in higgledy-piggledy lives of hurting people, sharing the love that altered ours.

Lord God, what mercy You've shown me. How boundless the love that brought me to Your eternal kingdom.

February 16

*Woe to those who plan iniquity, to those who plot
evil on their beds! . . . The Lord says, "I am
planning disaster against this people, from which
you cannot save yourselves."*
MICAH 2:1, 3

How can Mr. Raynes live with himself?" Trisha
wanted to know. "He's laying off thousands of work-
ers, after he gave himself a huge bonus last year!"

"Finding a new job may not be easy for most
of them," Bart added.

"It's just not fair," Louise agreed.

A few years later, Trisha began to see God's
faithfulness, despite her boss's frailties. She ran
into Louise in a mall and found that her friend had
a great part-time job that gave her more time with
her growing children. Bart had started his own
successful business.

"I hear Mr. Raynes is having a hard time hiring
people now," Louise added. "His company isn't
doing all that well because so many people know
about some of his financial dealings. Seems he
wasn't honest in other areas, too, and lost a few
clients. He got just what he gave others right back
at him."

Like Trisha, you may not see God working justice in your world, but hold on—He's always in
control.

*Thank You, Father God, for Your justice that never
fails.*

February 17

*"Blessed are ye, when men shall hate you,
and when they shall separate you from their
company, and shall reproach you, and cast out
your name as evil, for the Son of man's sake."*
LUKE 6:22, KJV

Sandy hurt when her best friend, Linda, wouldn't listen as she tried to tell her about Jesus. Sandy had just begun to experience a wonderful relationship with God and wanted to share it.

Being rejected was bad enough, but when she found out that Linda had started saying she was part of a cult, Sandy's heart ached. How could her best friend misunderstand her so?

In prayer, Sandy asked God, *How could this happen?* Then she opened her devotional, and the reading for the day was today's text.

Like Sandy, all of us have friends or family who misunderstand our faith. That doesn't mean there's anything wrong with us. We aren't necessarily saying the wrong words when we witness. From early in His ministry, Jesus warned us that people won't always accept our testimony.

But God can turn even rejection into a blessing.

Because of her friend's attitude, Sandy found some new friends—Christians—and one of them led Linda to Jesus.

Jesus, I want to share You with friends and family. Touch their hearts and open them to Your Word.

February 18

*"Whoever has my commands and obeys them,
he is the one who loves me."*
JOHN 14:21

Betty Ann loved the Lord, but she had a hard time loving one coworker, Doris. No matter when Betty Ann took lunch, Doris was hanging around, waiting to complain about how terrible life was.

One day, despite her irritation, Betty Ann clearly felt the Spirit's pull to share her faith with Doris. Horrified, she did something she'd never done before—she refused to witness.

I just can't, Lord, she prayed. *My church has enough troubles without adding* her *to them. Imagine if she wanted to go to church with me!*

Betty Ann never did witness to Doris. Instead she went out to lunch every day to avoid her.

A week later, Doris got another job and left the company.

Betty Ann felt awful. She'd knowingly disobeyed God's command, and she could never forget that. Her failure burned into Betty Ann's soul. She confessed her sin and prayed someone else would have the courage to witness to Doris.

Disobedience always has a painful price. Don't ruin your love for Jesus by ignoring His voice.

Lord, keep me from disobedience and make my love for You grow each day.

February 19

On your way to work, your car suddenly gives you trouble. You know it's practically hung together with rubber bands, but why did it have to break down *now?* Finally you call a towing service or find a garage.

While you wait for service, do you worry about the work piling up on your desk? Or perhaps you're thinking of the grief your boss will give you when you finally do get in. If you have a long wait, your blood may simmer.

The mechanic's attitude makes a huge difference. If he's helpful and tries to get you on the road quickly, your blood pressure drops again. But if his attitude says *I'll get to it when I can,* you may be furious when you leave—and you won't come to that unwise businessman again.

Every day, you're like that mechanic. You can give God good, positive service or surly responses. Are you a servant He looks forward to using?

I want to be a wise servant who glorifies You, Lord, not one with an attitude that reflects badly on You. Keep me diligent in my labors.

February 20

*Then I heard the voice of the Lord saying,
"Whom shall I send? And who will go for us?"
And I said, "Here am I. Send me!"*
ISAIAH 6:8

Ever wish that you could rewrite that verse to say, "Here am I, send someone else"? When you feel overloaded spiritually, even though you'd like to comply, opening yourself to full obedience to God is hard.

Maybe, you worry, *if I give Him free rein, He'll send me to Timbucktu* (or wherever your least-favorite place in the world is). *How could I ever cope with that?* you wonder.

If you're feeling overloaded, take your burden to God and confess that you've been hanging on to it. Then drop it in His hands and run! Don't stick around to pull it back out of the hands of the great burden lifter.

Then let Him lead you as you make decisions about ministries with which you're overinvolved, family problems that someone else needs to handle, or commitments you may not need to take on.

Pledge yourself to obedience, and walk in your new freedom. Don't let that old burden trap you again!

Send me, Lord, wherever You want me to go. I know You'll give me the strength I need.

February 21

Every wise woman buildeth her house:
but the foolish plucketh it down with her hands.
PROVERBS 14:1, KJV

Wilma's marriage wasn't going at all well. She and Kevin never seemed to talk anymore, unless it was to quarrel. Wilma did talk to Kathy, though, who heard all her troubles.

One day, Wilma told Kathy about a guy at work. "I think he's interested in me, which is more than I can say for Kevin," she admitted.

Shocked, Kathy warned her against becoming involved. "Seek out counseling. I'm sure you can work it out with Kevin," she advised her friend. "If you give up too easily on your marriage, you may regret it for the rest of your life."

Some people seem to destroy their relationships with their own hands. They make unwise decisions, based on what they want today, without looking at the effects those choices will have on the future. A few years down the road, they're in trouble and wondering why.

The bricks and stones from God's Word give us the wisdom that builds a house no one can destroy—not even ourselves.

Savior, I want to build a strong, happy home, not one based on Satan's lies. As I study Your Word, show me the choices I need to make.

February 22

A cheerful look brings joy to the heart, and good news gives health to the bones.
Proverbs 15:30

You've heard the saying, "When Mama ain't happy, ain't nobody happy." There's a lot of truth to that saying, because one person can easily change the attitude of a whole family—whether it's the mother or someone else.

At home, a mother has a lot of emotional sway, but it's the same in a church, office, or another gathering of people. One complainer can do a lot of harm. One person with a grudge can spread it around in a matter of minutes.

As a Christian, you have no excuse for becoming a whiner and complainer. Instead of destroying an office atmosphere, brighten it up with a smile. Share some good things that are going on (or the Good News of Jesus) on your lunch hour.

That way people won't want to avoid you— they'll decide you're healthy to be around.

Lord, even when I don't have a lot of good news, help me stay positive. After all, I have the best news in the world—that You died to save sinners like me.

February 23

*And let us consider how we may spur
one another on toward love
and good deeds.*
HEBREWS 10:24

A church member does a favor for you—something that takes him out of his way or takes extra effort. How do you respond? Can you assume that because you are fellow Christians, you don't even have to give a thank you in return? Or do you have to give exactly as much as he gave you?

Ignoring a brother's thoughtfulness will not spur him on to good deeds. But turning a favor into a tit-for-tat situation won't make the deed any more pleasant, either.

When another Christian does something nice, thank her. Tell her what it meant to you. Later, if you have a chance to help her out, by all means do so. But don't make her uncomfortable by falling all over yourself to return the favor.

Instead, pass on that good deed to another. After all, someone else may really need help, and you may be just the one who can give it.

Eventually God evens up all this giving business and everyone benefits.

Lord, when a fellow Christian does a good deed for me, help me to be thankful, then humble enough to pass on the good I've received.

February 24

Jesus asked, "Do you see anything?"
He looked up and said, "I see people;
they look like trees walking around."
MARK 8:23–24

I f you are nearsighted, you can relate to this man. Step outdoors without your glasses, and you may see trees as if they were covered by water.

Poor vision isn't hard to correct. You visit a doctor and get glasses or contact lenses. In a short while, you're 20/20.

But many of us with good eyesight don't recognize another kind of blindness—the moral kind. Even Christians can fall into this trap. Tempted by lust, we make excuses: *It's okay as long as I only go so far.* Or, *Well, we plan on getting married anyway.* We don't take a good look at the Good Book and we ignore the clear commands written there. Fuzzy moral vision keeps us from knowing the truth.

Doubtful moral choices can make you feel uncomfortable deep in your heart. Peace seems elusive, and life is hard.

Feel that way? Maybe the soul doctor is trying to get your attention. Turn to the Great Physician to clear your vision.

O Great Physician, heal my moral sight. I want to see Your will 20/20 and walk in it every day.

February 25

*"Come unto me, all ye that labour and
are heavy laden, and I will give you rest."*
MATTHEW 11:28, KJV

When you start on heavy labor—helping a friend move into his new place or digging in a garden—you work freely. It seems easy. But as you begin to tire, you set a goal: *I'll do this much, then take a rest.* Later, your muscles feel the strain, and thoughts of a break fill your mind. Finally, you just have to stop working. It's the same with emotional or spiritual work. You can't go on forever without Jesus' rest.

When you're working forty hours a week, hitting the mall after work, involved in ministry, and visiting friends on the weekend, by the time you get home, you're pooped. Your Bible sits unused on your nightstand. Next morning, you scramble to the office, and a quiet time just doesn't seem to fit in.

Life's too hectic, you think.

Well, of course it is! You missed the first part of this verse and didn't come to Jesus.

Lord, each day I need to come to You in prayer and through the Scriptures. When I'm feeling too busy, draw me with Your Spirit. I need to schedule a meeting with You.

February 26

"But when you pray, go into your room, close the door and pray to your Father, who is unseen."
MATTHEW 6:6

Time got away from Amy that morning, and prayer seemed out of the question. Jumping in her car, she decided, *I'll just pray while I drive.*

As she started off, so did her prayer, but soon she got caught in traffic. Faced with the choice of having an accident or prayer, she kept her mind on the road. Past the traffic, Amy turned again to prayer, only to lose track again when she saw a *Sale* sign on one of her favorite stores.

Sure, you *can* pray while you drive—maybe you *should* sometimes—but if that's the only time you spend with God, you won't be giving Him your best. After all, two seconds of prayer here and a minute there can't compete with solid time when God can answer you.

If you only talked to your friends while you drove, you couldn't give them your full attention, and your communication would get mixed up. It's the same with God.

Lord, I know I can pray when I drive, but there are too many distractions to make it my prayer room. My life includes time to spend with You. Show me when it is.

February 27

But Joshua had commanded the people,
"Do not give a war cry,
do not raise your voices,
do not say a word until the day
I tell you to shout. Then shout!"
JOSHUA 6:10

I magine—Joshua thinks we'll take the city just by shouting! you can almost hear some doubters thinking when they hear these words. *What good does he think that will do against city walls and soldiers?* they must have added. But the people did as Joshua said, and amazingly, the walls did fall. God destroyed the city.

Sometimes God asks us to do things doubters don't understand. When we live according to His Word, plenty of people think we, too, are unrealistic. We may even be accused of being Pollyannas because we try to do good.

But obeying by faith, not following reason alone, is the heart of the gospel. Anyone can follow the world's plan that says, "I'll believe it when I see it." Holding on and doing God's will when it looks silly takes strength.

As they walked into Jericho, the Israelites didn't look silly, did they?

Lord, sometimes my mind tells me not to obey You when Your commands "just don't make sense." Teach my spirit to follow Your call.

February 28

In those days there was no king in Israel: every man did that which was right in his own eyes.
JUDGES 21:25, KJV

That one sentence speaks volumes about Israel.

Over and over God had rescued His people. After moving into the Promised Land, Israel had seen Him defend them against the pagan nations. What more proof could they have wanted that their God was worthy of obedience? But by the end of the time of the judges, disorder ruled their souls—and their country.

When we resist God again and again, eventually rebellion burns deep into our souls. Though God has shown His mercy, we can no longer see it. We're abusing Him, so He finally gives us our just desserts.

That's what He did to Israel. Finally tired of their own misrule, Israel demanded a king, just like the other—pagan—nations. They wanted to become copycats of those who didn't love Him, so God gave them Saul—a copycat king who made them suffer in the same way pagan kings abused their people.

Don't put a Saul in charge of *your* life—give control to the Lord who rescued Israel instead.

Jesus, I don't want to fall into a pattern of rebellion. Show me the sins I tend to repeat and cleanse them from my life.

February 29

And the sun stood still, and the moon stayed,
until the people had avenged themselves
upon their enemies. . . . So the sun stood still
in the midst of heaven, and hasted not
to go down about a whole day.
JOSHUA 10:13, KJV

Amazing—at a time when they needed it, God gave Israel an extra full day of light! The sun and the moon cooperated with humanity's need, because God declared it.

We can't explain how it happened. Used to the regular rising of the sun and moon, we can't imagine things any other way—and it must have also astonished the Amorites, whom Israel was attacking. Instead of getting away under the cover of night, they had to keep fighting.

Today we have an extra day that only comes once every four years. Unlike the Amorites, we don't get it as a total surprise.

How do we use this extra twenty-four hours? Will it be a blessing to us and others or something that's just lost in the sauce of another year?

Every day is important. God doesn't have to stop time to make it so.

How will you use today?

Thank You, Lord, for another day to serve You. I want to make the most of it by showing someone Your love.

March 1

*May you be richly rewarded by the LORD,
the God of Israel, under whose wings you
have come to take refuge.*
RUTH 2:12

This blessing was given to Ruth, who trusted the God of Israel as she went with her mother-in-law to a land far from her home. Many people face a similar dilemma today. They move away to accept a job that isn't available in their hometown, leaving friends and family behind. In the meantime, their parents grow older, until eventually they can no longer live independently and their children face a hard decision. How should they care for their parents? Should they uproot themselves or their parents?

There is no "correct" answer. Every family is different, and no solution is perfect. This isn't a problem you have to deal with immediately, but you should think about it now and talk it over with your parents. You need to know what they want; they need to know what you feel willing and able to do when the time comes. You all need to know that God will spread His wings and protect you when you look to Him for help.

Father, thank You for Your help and protection. When I have to make these difficult decisions, give me the guidance I need.

March 2

But as for you, be strong and do not give up,
for your work will be rewarded.
2 CHRONICLES 15:7

How do you know what God wants you to do? If you think you know, how can you be sure you're not acting out of your own desires instead of God's? Sometimes God seems to be pushing you one way; the next day you feel as if you're on your own.

Doing God's will is a long-term project. You may start out in one direction and get sidetracked. A roadblock may suddenly appear ahead of you, forcing a detour you didn't expect. A door of opportunity you never knew existed may open right in front of you. Our paths seem to travel more like a sailboat than a powerboat. We tack from one direction to another, not making much forward progress.

Eventually you'll know where you're going. Your road will suddenly feel right, and you'll see signs of your destination on the horizon.

So tack if you have to, but never give up seeking to do God's will for your life.

Father, thank You for the guidance You give me. Although my progress may seem slow, I know You will get me where I'm supposed to be.

March 3

*In everything that he undertook
in the service of God's temple and
in obedience to the law and the commands,
he sought his God and worked wholeheartedly.
And so he prospered.*
2 CHRONICLES 31:21

King Hezekiah was totally committed to the service of God, seeking His will and working wholeheartedly. As a result, he prospered. Should we expect anything less if we commit our lives to God and wholeheartedly follow His will?

The Bible doesn't say that Hezekiah had an easy time of it. If you read his whole story, you'll see he worked harder than today's corporate leaders ever do. There must have been days when he was sick of all the organizing, rebuilding, defending, and other chores that fall on a king. He'd solve one problem only to have six others appear. Hezekiah wasn't perfect, either. He and the whole kingdom were punished for their pride when Hezekiah neglected to give God the glory for a miracle.

He must have been a wise man to rule successfully for twenty-nine years. But remember, Hezekiah was twenty-five when he became king!

Lord, teach me to seek Your will with all my heart and do it with the wisdom and enthusiasm of Hezekiah, the young king who was rewarded for his faithfulness.

March 4

The sleep of a labouring man is sweet,
whether he eats little or much:
but the abundance of the rich
will not suffer him to sleep.
ECCLESIASTES 5:12, KJV

Why can't a rich man sleep well? There's too much to worry about. A person without money to invest in the stock market never has to look at the financial pages. He can go straight to the sports pages without guilt. Someone who lives in an apartment never has to worry about the grass or the tree branch hanging over the roof. A dink in an old car is nothing to worry about; one in a BMW has to be fixed, at great expense.

People with money usually end up buying themselves problems. Make no mistake, being rich is a lot of work and worry.

"We should all have it so bad," you may be thinking, but there's something to be said for a simple lifestyle. You can appreciate the sunset just as much in a rowboat as on a yacht.

Father, help me be content, whatever style of life my paycheck provides. I know You will see to my daily needs.

March 5

He repays a man for what he has done;
he brings upon him what
his conduct deserves.
JOB 34:11

God's rewards vary from person to person. There isn't one big, specific reward we are all competing for, which makes sense, since all our hopes and dreams are different, and so are what we consider to be good rewards.

Sometimes God doesn't just hand us our rewards —we have to find them. It's not that God is playing games with us. He just knows that a little effort on our part will make us appreciate our rewards all the more. So the next time your life seems to be all work and no fun, look under a few bushes and discover the surprises God has waiting for you.

O Lord, You care for every part of my life and know me inside out. Although some of my rewards may be hidden right now, I am confident You will help me find them.

March 6

Work brings profit,
but mere talk leads to poverty!
PROVERBS 14:23, NLT

This verse sounds an awful lot like a notice tacked up next to the water cooler at work. While management and employees may differ on the definition of "mere talk," a good amount of work can be done over one coffee break. Getting to know a new employee or sharing a joke with someone from another department can be profitable and proper. When the discussion is over, we return to work a little better connected to those with whom we work.

Then there's actual "mere talk," which wastes time and can cost you your job. Stopping to chat with a new employee is a gracious gesture; spending an hour filling him or her in on all the office gossip is mere talk. If you are having difficulty getting your assigned work done on time, keep track of the time you waste each day in such conversations and make the necessary adjustments.

Let my words be only those that glorify You, Lord,
and keep my tongue from mere talk.

March 7

*"Stop judging by mere appearances,
and make a right judgment."*
JOHN 7:24

Our whole country is caught up in appearance today, almost to the point of making it an idol. We are consumed by the desire to be thin, to be beautiful, to dress with flair and style. All of these may be perfectly legitimate personal goals, but we can all too easily pervert them, try to impose them on others, and then judge everyone who doesn't measure up as unworthy.

Today the fit mock those who puff their way up the stairs. The beautiful recommend nose jobs. The tall look down on the small; those who look as if they need a good sandwich feel superior to those who have obviously had too many.

Jesus tells us to look beyond the surface, to judge actions, not appearances. We have no right to make our personal preferences the basis for judging the worthiness of others.

Father, just as I don't want to be judged by my acceptance of some popular trend, neither do I want to judge others by my own personal preferences. Keep me sensitive to the feelings of others and help me see the true person beyond the surface.

March 8

For, brethren, ye have been called unto liberty; only use not liberty for an occasion to the flesh.
GALATIANS 5:13, KJV

Political scientists say that constant vigilance is the price of liberty. Someone born free must take an active part in maintaining freedom, or rights will slowly be eroded away and freedom will fail.

The same is true in our personal lives. We are largely free to do what we please, within limits. Some of these limits are enforced by laws we've all supported since the Ten Commandments were handed down. Other limits are man-made for the good of society and are more open to quibbling. But, in general, we're pretty free.

This freedom requires constant vigilance. We are responsible for our personal lives. We have to watch our standards, obey the laws God made for our conduct, and recognize sin when we see it. Our God-given freedom must be protected, not abused.

Lord, help me use my personal freedom wisely and take responsibility for all my actions.

March 9

The laborer's appetite works for him;
his hunger drives him on.
PROVERBS 16:26

The days of working in one place for a lifetime are long gone. Today a young person faces a long series of jobs in several fields, no pension plan to count on, a tottering Social Security system, and variable medical coverage.

Your parents may not have made anything near what you're making today, but they had a lot more job security and the opportunity to retire and enjoy life a little. You have to save and invest like mad. The rules have changed, and you have to learn the new rules early.

The good part is that you may find more job satisfaction than your parents ever did, rise higher, make more, and lead a longer, more fulfilling life. Appetite drives us to achieve more than we ever thought possible.

Thank You, Lord, for providing me with the motivation I need to succeed. I appreciate that You provide a way for me to feed myself. Challenge me to be the best I can be.

March 10

To the man who pleases him,
God gives wisdom, knowledge and happiness,
but to the sinner he gives the task of
gathering and storing up wealth to
hand it over to the one who pleases God.
ECCLESIASTES 2:26

Wisdom, knowledge, and happiness are the rewards of those who please God. These rewards come directly from God, with no one in between. What goes around comes around, and the sinner ends up with nothing.

Sometimes life doesn't seem to work this way, but a lot goes on that we don't see, and we have to take the Lord's word for it, because this is a long-term promise.

More important, this verse helps us set our priorities. Our most important task is pleasing God with the way we live. If we do this, the rewards will follow. God Himself will provide us with the wisdom, knowledge, and happiness we need, and financial rewards will follow from them.

Sin, on the other hand, has no long-term rewards at all.

Father, I want to please You with my life. If my actions result in rewards, I will be thankful for them, but living my life according to Your wishes is the greatest reward of all.

March 11

Two are better than one,
because they have a good return for their work:
If one falls down, his friend can help him up.
But pity the man who falls and
has no one to help him up!
ECCLESIASTES 4:9–10

The old buddy system you learned at summer camp was a pain in the neck. The whistle would blow and you'd have to hold up your joined hands to show you were there to save your buddy, if needed. Even though it cramped your style, it was sort of nice to see your buddy was right where he was supposed to be. It made swimming lessons seem safer.

Even adults need the buddy system. You need at least one person you can trust at work. If you're into outdoor activities, you know better than to wander off into the woods alone. And when you're suffering from loneliness, life is much more bearable if you have someone you can call in the middle of the night.

How glad I am when I can share some of my burdens with others. Give me the opportunity to be a "buddy" to someone who needs my help or a listening ear.

March 12

*Unto the pure all things are pure: but unto them
that are defiled and unbelieving is nothing pure;
but even their mind and conscience is defiled.*
TITUS 1:15, KJV

A Christian looks at life with a lot more hope than a non-Christian. Sure, the world is full of sin, but a Christian should be willing to give everyone the benefit of a doubt. We slip, too, and it's not our job to judge others. In general, a Christian wants to see the good in everything and everyone.

Those without faith see the world as a dark, dangerous place where might makes right. Since they see everything as wicked, why should they be good? In fact, they soon come to believe there is no difference at all between good and bad—their consciences become corrupted.

It's pretty obvious which worldview is most common today. Do you have the courage to think like a Christian? You'll be in the minority. You'll be called a fool, or at least naive. But you'll be happy.

*Father, I don't want to see the world through the
eyes of the unfaithful. Your world is good. You put
it here for us to enjoy. Give me the courage to love
Your world and everything in it.*

March 13

Though you have not seen him, you love him;
and even though you do not see him now,
you believe in him and are filled with
an inexpressible and glorious joy.
1 PETER 1:8

You have never seen Jesus, yet your belief in Him and love for Him are so strong that they fill you with "inexpressible and glorious joy." This is the wonder of faith.

Faith plays a part in your love of others, too, especially in the search for a husband or wife. Somewhere out there is the person you were meant to marry. You've never seen him—and he's certainly not in sight now—but you believe he's there, and this belief fills you with joy. Maybe you have a mental image of what he'll look like, maybe not. Certainly you know what he will act like: warm, compassionate, funny, faithful. He's there, somewhere, and you love him already, although you've never even seen him.

He's not perfect, though, and you need to keep that in mind. He's not Jesus. Don't confuse your hunger for the Lord with your hunger for human love.

Father, my love for Jesus gives me a taste of the human love I am looking for. Help me find the one You have in mind for me.

March 14

With the tongue we praise our Lord and Father,
and with it we curse men,
who have been made in God's likeness.
Out of the same mouth come praise and cursing.
My brothers, this should not be.
JAMES 3:9–10

Most of us speak before thinking. It's automatic, out of our control—or so it seems. We use words today that our mothers would have washed our mouths out for using. Stand-up comedians and movie characters use these words so often that they lose all their meaning and eventually fail to shock us at all.

But the phrase "dirty mouth" has a real meaning. Would you take communion with filthy hands? Of course not. It would be sacrilegious. Would you pick up a toddler and tell him a dirty joke? You wouldn't think of it. And yet we take our dirty mouths to church and sing God's praises with them!

If we are going to try to be holy, we have to be aware of what we say, as well as what we do.

Lord, help me gain control of my tongue, so others who hear what I say will be drawn to You and not be put off by my thoughtless words.

March 15

"Take heed, and beware of covetousness: for a man's life consisteth not in the abundance of the things which he possesseth."
LUKE 12:15, KJV

Abundance of possessions isn't a big problem for a young person starting off. Lack of possessions is much more likely to be the problem. A person isn't being greedy when he wants a car to get to work or a new suit for a job interview, but if the car has to be a Mercedes and the suit Italian-made, that's edging into greediness.

In the same way, wanting to succeed is not greed. Ambition is God's way of prodding us into action. But devoting yourself to success day and night, forsaking everything else in the climb to the top—well, that's greed.

As Jesus said, there are all kinds of greed to watch out for. Sometimes it's hard to tell when you've gone over the line. The next time you think you may be falling into greediness, give yourself the "tombstone test." How do you want to be remembered?

Father, help me distinguish between ambition and greed. Show me the right choices in how to use my talents and blessings.

March 16

The pastures will soon be green.
JOEL 2:22, NLT

Spring is almost here, though in some places you would never know it. Seed ordered in the middle of winter is arriving, and those who like an early crop of spinach or peas are turning over a spade full of soil in hopes it's dry enough to plant. It's probably not, but just the act of getting out there and checking is enough to give you a lift.

At least now you can pick up all those sticks littering the yard and clean up the perennial bed. Those living in apartments may not be able to do any of this, but a new houseplant or two in a sunny window gives the same effect, as does a walk through the park.

We're not as connected to the soil as our forefathers were, but the hope that spring brings still bubbles inside us, a memory engraved on our souls. It's time to get outside and look for little green shoots. After a long, dreary winter, even a patch of skunk cabbage is a promise of summer.

Father, thank You for the promise of spring and the happiness it brings. Remind me to take the time to look for it today.

March 17

Does the hawk take flight by your wisdom
and spread his wings toward the south?
Does the eagle soar at your command
and build his nest on high?
Job 39:26–27

There's a lot in our lives we can control and an awful lot we can't. Bosses and duties and family obligations hem us in, and sometimes we just want to shake them all off our backs and take control of ourselves again. Some Mondays we want to sleep until noon. Fat chance. Sleeping in on Mondays gets you fired, and being totally free is an impossible dream.

Even wild animals have laws they obey. How do birds know when it's time to migrate? Who shows an eagle the only safe place for her nest? Scientists have partial answers, but eventually they have to admit there's a lot they don't know about nature's laws.

If you've ever seen a salmon struggling against the current, scraping its skin against rocks and dodging bears hungry after a long winter fast, you'll have some appreciation of the freedom you *do* have.

Father, thank You for the choices I have in life. The next time I want to chuck it all, remind me my life is a lot better than most.

March 18

Fortunately, we're not responsible for everything. Can you just imagine some international commission being responsible for the world's rain? They'd try to be fair. They'd knock down mountains that collect rain on one side and block it from the other. They'd seed clouds over parched land and discover twenty years later that the seeding caused cancer. They'd even sponsor worldwide rain dances.

But they would fail. There would be wars when drought struck and revolutions when floods arrived, because *someone* would have to be punished for their failure. If you read any science fiction at all, you know that terraforming on a large scale brings more problems than it solves.

Better to leave some things to God, who knows what He's doing, even if we don't understand the whole process. We humans are a very adaptable species, and He is able to provide what we need.

Father, keep us from trying to control what only You understand. Our sciences bring us wonderful advances, but our world needs to be controlled by Your laws, not ours.

March 19

*Suppose a brother or sister is without clothes
and daily food. If one of you says to him,
"Go, I wish you well; keep warm and well fed,"
but does nothing about his physical needs,
what good is it?*
JAMES 2:15–16

T housands of people die of starvation every day, while we become the most overweight nation in the world. Our mechanized farming produces more food than we can possibly eat, while others are still using hand tools to scrape out a living.

What can one person do about such inequity? Perhaps the best thing is to try to think on a global scale, not a local one. Keeping a larger picture in mind makes it easy to recycle and get involved in environmental issues. "Adopting" a needy foster child in another country, doing volunteer work for a local charity, donating the extra clothes you really don't need to someone who does—these are all small efforts, but they do make a difference. You don't have to totally change your lifestyle to help the world.

Lord, make me understand what I can and cannot do to help others in the world today. Show me the small actions I can take that will make a difference.

March 20

The Lord is nigh unto them that are of a broken heart; and saveth such as be of a contrite spirit.
PSALM 34:18, KJV

You don't hear people talking about broken hearts these days, unless you are fond of country music, but they still happen to everyone at least once. You get dumped by someone you were seriously considering taking home to meet the folks. How could you have misread all the signals? How could something that seemed so good turn out to be a nightmare? What did you do?

Most of us turn into hermits for a while, dissecting the failed relationship over and over, trying to figure out what happened. Fortunately, friends put an end to that pretty soon, the unromantic fools. They drag you out of the apartment—or sit in it with you until you go out in self-defense. They tell you to get on with your life, and they fix you up. They nag you back into emotional health.

At the same time, God's doing a little work on you, too. Unlike your friends, He doesn't nag or fix you up. He's just there for you when you need Him, and He always understands.

Father, thank You for comforting me when I go and get my heart broken. I know if it happens again, You'll be there for me again.

March 21

*There hath no temptation taken you but such
as is common to man: but God is faithful,
who will not suffer you to be tempted above
that ye are able; but will with the temptation
also make a way to escape,
that ye may be able to bear it.*
1 CORINTHIANS 10:13, KJV

Temptations come in all sizes and shapes, from
the seven deadly sins to sneaking a second dessert
when you're home alone. As the verse above says,
temptation is common, and God has seen them all.
Even Jesus was tempted. It's not the temptation that
makes you a sinner—you have to give in to the
temptation to earn that label—and God is still in
control of how much temptation comes your way.
Better yet, as you begin to waver, He can show
you how to get out of the situation. So the next
time you are tempted to do something you don't
want to do (or something you *do* want to do),
thank God for His help and look for the solution
He has provided for you.

*Father, thank You for Your care whenever I'm
tempted. I know I will never be tempted beyond
what I can bear. You will give me the strength to
resist.*

March 22

I believed; therefore I said,
"I am greatly afflicted."
PSALM 116:10

There's no question that being a believer brings afflictions of various types—minor martyrdoms. In some countries, believers are still being murdered. In ours, the afflictions are more social than physical, but that doesn't make them any easier to bear.

Some believers feel called to witness to their faith through words, wearing their faith on their shirtsleeves. Even doing this gently can lead to social problems. Others prefer to act as examples, witnessing through their acts and deeds. In some places, this is acceptable; in others, it's not. Every time believers say something or show devotion, they're open to minor martyrdom.

But you have to do what you have to do. Affliction is not the worst thing in the world. You can be afflicted by a disease—even the common cold. You can be afflicted by ambition, poverty, war, or even a tyrant of a boss. Since afflictions will come to you anyway, why not suffer the afflictions of a believer and do some good along the way?

Father, give me courage in the face of all my afflictions. I know You will care for me in any situation, and I want to do Your work.

March 23

*"Restrain your voice from weeping
and your eyes from tears,
for your work will be rewarded,"*
declares the LORD.
JEREMIAH 31:16

Jeremiah always said exactly what he was told to say. He wasn't noted for being diplomatic or worrying about what others would think of his blunt words. In this case, he was saying, "Stop whining and get back to work. You'll get your reward eventually."

But eventually doesn't pay this month's rent, and we get impatient waiting for our rewards. We can have instant hamburgers, instant communication, instant friends. Why not instant rewards?

Jeremiah understood a lot about work, too. Nobody likes a crybaby employee who constantly complains about his work and its unfulfilling poverty wage. Those who go about their work cheerfully are much more likely to make a good impression and reap some rewards. Which type of worker would you prefer if you were the boss? Which type are you?

Father, help me be a cheerful worker who can patiently wait for my reward. Keep me pleasant to be near, not a complainer.

March 24

They shall not build, and another inhabit;
they shall not plant, and another eat:
for as the days of a tree are
the days of my people,
and mine elect shall long enjoy
the work of their hands.
ISAIAH 65:22, KJV

It's so frustrating to work hard and build something you'll never be able to enjoy. Maybe you spend your days tuning up cars you can't afford to own or roof houses that you will never be able to afford. It's not fair.

God promises it won't always be that way. His people will live long, happy lives and enjoy the benefits of their own work. Notice that the Bible doesn't say God will *give* His people everything they want. It says they will earn what they get.

The apostles worked to support themselves while they preached. Paul was a tentmaker by profession. As he traveled the world, he must have spent many nights inside tents he had made himself. A number of the apostles were fishermen who fed themselves through their own work on the Sea of Galilee. In order to enjoy the works of your hand, first you have to do the work.

Father, thank You for caring for my needs every day. I promise to do my part, too.

March 25

I have labored to no purpose;
I have spent my strength in vain and for nothing.
Yet what is due me is in the LORD's hand,
and my reward is with my God.
ISAIAH 49:4

Some days you just can't win. The suit you just got back from the cleaner has mud on the cuff. Your cat turned over the goldfish bowl and ate the body. You said something at work, and the silence that followed made you want to creep under a desk. Nothing went right all day.

Doesn't anyone care that you had a rotten day and need a little encouragement? Well, you could call home and get some sympathy, but then you'd have to explain why you haven't been home for three months.

Why not just talk it out with God? He listens without comment. He knows exactly what kind of day you had, and He weeps for you. He's there, and He cares.

Even if no one seems to appreciate me, I know that You do, Lord. In just a second, my day can become holy when I reach out to You.

March 26

Maybe you're thinking you don't care who you report to as long as the check comes every week, but experience will change your mind. Who you report to does make a difference. A change in your supervisor often means a promotion, a chance to have your opinions heard by someone with the power to put plans in action. It can mean the assignment of real responsibility.

You can get there by at least two paths: office politics or good work. Often the political route seems to work the fastest, especially at the lower levels. Some people rise like balloons until they hit the peak of their ability and explode. They can't handle the work.

The safest way to succeed is to rise slowly but surely on the basis of what you can do. You go up a level, learn the job at hand, and prove you can do more. Then it's safe to reach for another rung on the ladder.

Father, help me learn one job at a time and build my future on what I can do, not my ability to "look good."

March 27

I am in the midst of lions;
I lie among ravenous beasts—
men whose teeth are spears and arrows,
whose tongues are sharp swords.
PSALM 57:4

Does this sound like a description of your neighborhood? Does your apartment have bars over the windows and your door at least three locks? Do you come home from work and stay inside from dusk to dawn? In many places, this is the only safe way to live, and you have to deal with it.

You also have to rise above it, to refuse to be a prisoner in your own home. You can join other neighbors and help take back the streets. You can stay in the neighborhood when you have the money to get out. You can volunteer to be a mentor, to help a neighborhood sports program—to invest yourself and your money where it will make a difference.

It's not easy, but Psalm 57:7 says, "My heart is steadfast, O God, my heart is steadfast; I will sing and make music." Make music wherever you live.

Father, it's tempting to get out as soon as possible and leave all these problems behind me. Give me the strength to make music in places where there is only discord and trouble.

March 28

God wants you to be holy,
so you should keep clear of all sexual sin.
Then each of you will control your body
and live in holiness and honor—
not in lustful passion as the pagans do,
in their ignorance of God and his ways.
1 THESSALONIANS 4:3–5, NLT

Avoiding sexual immorality does not come naturally—it has to be *learned*—and there are very few teachers you can count on today. Society at large is pretty useless, issuing plenty of warnings about disease but little positive, practical advice for those struggling to lead a sanctified life.

So who is available to teach these lessons? The best teacher is God Himself, who can teach you what He expects through the Bible. Use a good concordance to look up verses about sex, love, marriage, and so forth. You can't obey laws you don't know exist, but all the laws are there in the Bible. Besides knowledge, God can give you the strength you will need to control your own body and live a pure life. Ask for His help when you need it.

Father, thank You for guiding me in all things. Forgive me when I disappoint You, and give me the strength I need to please You.

March 29

And what does the LORD require of you?
To act justly and to love mercy
and to walk humbly with your God.
MICAH 6:8

What does God expect of His people? That's Micah's question. Should they bring Him burned offerings, thousands of rams, rivers of oil? Should they offer their firstborn children as payment for their sins? What will please the God who has saved them? How can they possibly repay such a debt?

The answer is to act justly, love mercy, and walk humbly with God. Whew! Is that it? What a relief!

Well, yes, it does sound pretty easy. But when you get down to specifics, it involves a total life change. In an unjust world, we are to be just. In a day when might makes right, we are to love mercy. In a life where we need to be our own public-relations person to get ahead, we are required to be humble. And while others follow the lead of movie stars, we are to walk with God.

Father, thank You for all You have done for me. I know I can never repay You with any offering less than my whole life. Help me to be just, merciful, and humble in my daily walk with You.

March 30

I am on the verge of collapse,
facing constant pain.
But I confess my sins;
I am deeply sorry for what I have done.
PSALM 38:17–18, NLT

Jesus was the only perfect person in the world. David, who wrote the verses above, was as sinful as the next man, yet God favored him over all other kings and chose his descendants to be the earthly ancestors of Jesus.

God knows we will sin. It's in our nature to do so. Not that we can use that as an excuse, but it is a fact of life we have to live with. God meant us to live happy lives, not be weighed down by an unnatural burden of sin. Jesus has accepted that burden for us. Give it over to Him, accept His sacrifice with joy, go on with your life, and try to sin no more.

Father, thank You for forgiving all my sins through Your Son, Jesus Christ. Let me dwell on what You have done for me, not on the many ways I have failed You.

March 31

One generation will commend your works to another; they will tell of your mighty acts. They will speak of the glorious splendor of your majesty, and I will meditate on your wonderful works.
PSALM 145:4–5

There was no Internet in the days of David, no instant communication. Most people couldn't read or write. Traditions were taught to a young generation by the older generation, often through stories, songs, and dances, which were memorable and enjoyable ways to learn. The psalms and hymns of the church not only lift people's spirits but serve as teaching tools.

Perhaps you were not cut out to be a witness. The thought of speaking to another person about your beliefs may scare you into silence. But there are other ways to communicate. Can you tell stories? Can you sing? Can you dance? Can you draw? Faith and the joy it brings you can be communicated through many means. Offer God the talents you do have, and He will find a way to use them.

Father, show me how I can tell others about Your mighty works and pass on the faith I treasure. You know what I am capable of, and I do want to help.

April 1

And as they sat and did eat, Jesus said,
"Verily I say unto you,
One of you which eateth with me
shall betray me."
And they began to be sorrowful,
and to say unto him one by one,
"Is it I?" and another said, "Is it I?"
MARK 14:18–19, KJV

Just the kind of firm believers you'd like to have following you if you were about to face the cross, right? Twelve men who aren't even sure of their own hearts!

Told that one would betray Jesus, for a single honest moment, not one disciple—not even brash Peter—guaranteed *he* would never give in.

But Jesus used these less-than-confident men precisely because they recognized their own weakness. God doesn't look for self-sufficient disciples who never err. He looks for those who know they are weak and know whom to turn to—Jesus.

If you're facing trouble and feel you lack strength to stand firm, don't waste your time worrying; turn to Jesus instead. You're in exactly the right place.

Lord Jesus, I'm so weak that sometimes I don't even realize it. When I face a cross, I can trust only in You.

April 2

Those who passed by hurled insults at him,
shaking their heads and saying,
"So! You who are going to destroy
the temple and build it in three days,
come down from the cross and save yourself!"
MARK 15:29–30

Not only did Jesus suffer the physical pain of crucifixion, the taunts of these uncaring, unbelieving men rang in His ears.

Wasn't it enough that Jesus faced death? You'd think that alone could curb His enemies' tongues. Yet here were "religious" men jeering at a dying man (v. 31).

Fired by Satan, the intense hatred of the chief priests and teachers of the law left no space for compassion. They figured they had "won" and never recognized that this temple, God's Son, *was* being destroyed—and *they* were the destroyers.

The taunts must have angered Jesus' gentle heart. But seeking revenge would have wrecked God's ordained sacrifice and our deliverance. Had He come down from the cross for a few jeers, we would have been lost.

His humiliation meant our salvation.

How can it be, Lord Jesus, that You faced such humiliation for me? Without such love, I'd never know heaven's joys.

April 3

Again the high priest asked him,
and said unto him, "Art thou the Christ,
the Son of the Blessed?"
MARK 14:61, KJV

Even the high priest was confused by Jesus. How could *this* man be Messiah?

Maybe Caiaphas expected a military leader like Judah Maccabeus. During the second century B.C., Judah and his brothers had briefly freed most of Jerusalem from Syrian rule. A Messiah who could *keep* Jerusalem free would have been to the high priest's liking. A military man who wouldn't make the high priest give up his power would have perfectly suited Caiaphas's expectations.

Jesus just didn't fit the high priest's "Messiah picture." Even after three years of His ministry, Caiaphas had a hard time believing He was right for the "job."

This Easter, what is your "Messiah picture"? Do you want One who fights battles in your life—but won't expect you to give up control of it? If so, like Caiaphas, you probably have a different picture from the one in Scripture.

Get a perfect picture today—His name is Jesus, and He wants to be Lord of your whole life.

Jesus, I don't want to share Caiaphas's picture of You. Be King of my heart and rule my whole life.

April 4

So she came running to Simon Peter and the other disciple, the one Jesus loved, and said, "They have taken the Lord out of the tomb, and we don't know where they have put him!"
JOHN 20:2

This wasn't just a bad hair day for the disciples. No, it was the end of the most wretched weekend in their lives.

Their Messiah had been dragged in front of the religious authorities and tried in a kangaroo court. No religious authority could sentence Jesus to death—Roman law controlled a man's life. But no Roman official had stood up to the priests. So the Master had been crucified.

Then Mary came to the tomb and found Him gone. Could a bad weekend get much worse?

Even Peter and John weren't of much help. The men merely glanced in the tomb and returned home. Heavyhearted, Mary stood crying at the last place she'd seen the Master—and saw what Peter and John missed: the resurrected Jesus.

Even on tearful days—those "bottom ten" in your life, seek Him. Sorrow turns to joy when the resurrected Jesus touches a sad heart.

Like Mary, I want to keep seeking You, Jesus. My sorrows turn to joy when I come face-to-face with You.

April 5

*And how the chief priests and our rulers
delivered him to be condemned to death,
and have crucified him.
But we trusted that it had been he which
should have redeemed Israel.*
Luke 24:20–21, kjv

A few years ago, in New York, the disciples of an elderly Jewish rabbi began proclaiming he was Messiah. Not long after, the rabbi died. Hope ended shortly after that rabbi's life. After all, how could an eternal God have a dead Messiah?

Two disciples on their way to Emmaus felt the same pain. Cleopas and his friend thought their faith in Messiah had ended with the crucifixion. Hopelessness slowed their steps and sorrow filled their voices as they told the news to a chance-met "stranger."

This "stranger" showed them the truths of Scripture, and the disciples recognized Jesus. Hopelessness evaporated. They rushed back to Jerusalem to spread the Good News of the resurrection.

Does hopelessness blind you to Jesus' power in your life? Even when Easter is past on the calendar, it hasn't ended. Its promise lasts eternally for those who believe in Him.

Lord Jesus, keep the truth of Easter's promise in my heart the whole year. I need Your resurrecting power daily.

April 6

Once he went out on his own, Jared didn't seem to click with the local Christian young adults. So he made friends with some fellows he met at work.

At first they seemed like good guys. Al always said good things about his family, and Don was a hard worker. But one weekend, they asked Jared to a drinking party. At first he said no. But after a couple of lonely weekends, Jared went along "just for the ride." Al got drunk, and Jared felt disgusted. But a couple of weekends later all three friends were back at a similar party.

When he went home for Christmas and got tied up again with his church group, Jared realized the danger he'd put himself in. *What am I doing?* he asked himself. *I don't like drinking anyway.* He decided to look for some new, Christian friends, and he felt the Spirit warm his heart.

If, like Jared, you're flirting with sin, turn around today. Don't wait! The longer you stray, the harder it is to return to God.

Tempting as sin may be, help me resist it, Lord. I don't want to wake up one day and know I'm trapped.

April 7

*My purpose is that they may be encouraged
in heart and united in love, so that they
may have the full riches of complete
understanding, in order that they may
know the mystery of God, namely, Christ.*
COLOSSIANS 2:2

When it came to writing letters at work, Jane struggled. Nothing seemed to work. No matter how she tried, she always got more criticism than encouragement. Finally she asked Rachel, another Christian, to help her.

After reading her latest letters, Rachel pointed out that Jane was so busy using large words that her writing wasn't clear. "Say what you want to get across, not what you think will impress someone," she advised. Then Rachel turned to Colossians. "Paul didn't focus on himself when he wrote. He wrote things his readers could understand and learn from. You can make your message clear if you use this method, too."

The next time you write a letter, think first about the other person. What words will express what you want her to understand? How can you help him know your need? Then boot up your computer or pick up your pen.

Lord, when I communicate, I want to do it in a way that glorifies You, not me. Help me write clearly and lovingly.

April 8

*Some men came down from Judea to Antioch
and were teaching the brothers:
"Unless you are circumcised,
according to the custom taught by Moses,
you cannot be saved."*

ACTS 15:1

People—even some well-meaning Christians—
have a hard time accepting grace. They can't believe they don't have to add something to God's
work. So they set up rules and regulations: "You
have to do this, or you aren't a Christian." "You
don't really love God unless you do that."

The men in this verse were trying to follow the
Old Testament law as well as Jesus. They couldn't
accept that His blood had done it all and that,
when they accepted Him, their hearts, not their
bodies, were circumcised. Many serious Gentile
believers who wanted to obey God and feared setting a foot wrong did what these Judaizers said.
Fear led them into sin.

God doesn't want you to be afraid, to worry if
you've dotted all the *i*'s and crossed all the *t*'s that
will let you enter heaven.

No, He loved you, so He gave you a free gift,
no strings attached. Enjoy that gift today.

*Thank You, Jesus, for Your grace. You've done
everything that had to be done to bring me into
heaven. I want to give my life as thanks.*

April 9

*Thou wast he that leddest out and broughtest in
Israel: and the LORD thy God said unto thee,
"Thou shalt feed my people Israel,
and thou shalt be ruler over my people Israel."*
1 CHRONICLES 11:2, KJV

David waited a long time to hear the Hebrew people remember this promise made by God. Jesse's son carried this assurance in his heart as he became King Saul's general, ran from the crazed ruler and hid in the hills, and battled Israel's enemies from afar. Though he must have been tempted to believe God had forgotten His promise, David still trusted.

The ex-shepherd boy, who had learned patience watching sheep, knew God would be faithful. But when life got stressful, he must have wondered *when*. David wished no ill on Saul, but he must have speculated on God's timing.

Sometimes, like David, we've waited a long time for a much-needed change—we know we need a raise in order to keep up with our rent—or we long for the end of a troublesome family problem. Like David, we don't know where the solution will come from, but we know it *is* coming. After all, isn't David's faithful God our God, too?

Lord, I know You haven't forgotten me. Maybe I just need to get on Your timing. Give me patience to wait for Your best.

April 10

The words of Amos,
one of the shepherds of Tekoa—
what he saw concerning Israel. . .
AMOS 1:1

Look at plenty of books in Scripture, and you'll note they start with the writer's credentials. Paul always announced himself up front, and the prophets mention their names. Readers would have recognized the importance of these men.

Amos immediately identifies himself, but he wasn't a priest or a recognized prophet, and he hadn't even been sent to his own nation of Judah. If impressing the Israelites had been his first thought, Amos's chances were slim. Not too many folks were awed by men who raised woolly, dim-witted creatures; after all, it didn't take much sense to outwit a sheep. But the prophet didn't let people's opinions sway him. He spoke out as God had commanded.

God doesn't often work through the impressive people in our world. Sure, some Christians become well-known figures in politics or in their professions, but most don't get much fame.

That doesn't mean we can't still be faithful, like Tekoa's shepherd.

Lord, whether or not I impress people doesn't matter. All that counts is how much I've loved and served You. When I have the King of Kings as Savior, what more credentials do I need?

April 11

I will send you rain in its season,
and the ground will yield its crops
and the trees of the field their fruit.
LEVITICUS 26:4

It's April, and spring is either out in full force or on its way.

Spring means rain—gentle mists or furious downpours, complete with cats and dogs. Its gentle pleasure or irritating presence touches you.

When you've planned a day hiking and spring rain comes down in buckets, you probably forget God's seasonal plan. You want exercise, and the earth's renewal is the last thing on your mind. A fresh tomato or crisp autumn apple isn't in your thoughts. But God's kept them in mind. Only a few months down the road, He knows you'll be enjoying the fruit of this watering.

When delays bring life's plans to a halt—a friend can't rent an apartment with you or the ministry you've developed just falls through—remember, God has seasons in our lives, too. Through that disappointment, He is creating something you'll enjoy in the future. You may not understand it today, but a month or year later, you'll experience the benefits of the new growth He was watering.

Lord, I don't always see the fruit that's coming from my life. Make me bear good fruit in abundance.

April 12

Therefore, among God's churches we boast about your perseverance and faith in all the persecutions and trials you are enduring.
2 THESSALONIANS 1:4

Paul commended the Thessalonian Christians on their powerful faith, which had become the talk of the Christian world. The apostle boasted about them wherever he went.

Sure, you may be thinking. *I could be like that if I lived back then. It was easier for them.*

We'd like to think that. When our own witness seems weak, we assume others have it easier than we do. We excuse ourselves, *If only I had this. . .* Or, *If only I were older. . .* The *if onlys* could go on endlessly.

But the Thessalonians weren't armchair Christians. They suffered and endured trials. Many must have felt that being Christian wasn't always worth it.

Do we have to struggle so much? both we and the Thessalonians have wondered. *If only God would make our lives easier, couldn't we have a better witness?* we ask.

But trials and troubles are the tools God uses to develop His greatest saints.

Hold fast today!

Lord, some days the trials come raining down on me. No matter what my situation, let me be faithful to You.

April 13

*For there are many unruly
and vain talkers and deceivers.*
TITUS 1:10, KJV

Some of the smoothest talking Christians are the least effective people spiritually. Though they have plenty of words and arguments and may look like they have spirituality all under control, their lives miss God's touch if they lack an obedient and truthful spirit.

Nowhere in Scripture does God command us to speak perfectly before we share our faith. Neither Moses nor Paul claimed to have public speaking down pat, but how they talked didn't matter. The Lord wasn't looking for con men; He used these leaders powerfully because they were obedient.

A smooth talker may deceive people. But even the most rough-spoken person can show people truth—especially the truth about Jesus. It's not in the words, but the heart.

What do your words show about your heart?

Whether I'm a professional speaker or someone who hates to talk, my words need to be honest and gentle to reflect You, Jesus.

April 14

Even the laziest couch potato discovers energy after seeing one of those pricy fitness machines. Glimpse one, and you have visions of a new, sleeker you.

But once you try out these tempting machines, you learn it takes commitment and consistency to get that new figure. Before long, the machine becomes a place to drop your coat—but a clothes rack would have cost a whole lot less.

Coming to Jesus is something like buying exercise equipment. All you need to be successful is right there, ready to be used. But your Christian testimony won't automatically shine out in a dark world. That takes daily commitment and trust in God. Righteousness needs to be built up day by day.

Some people's Christian walk never goes further than their stroll down the aisle during an altar call. They don't want to change their lives. Those people are expensive clothes racks.

Seek out God every day through prayer, fellowship, and His Word, and you'll become a truly fit Christian.

Lord, I don't want to be useless to You. Make me fit for Your kingdom.

April 15

*"But so that we may not offend them,
go to the lake and throw out your line.
Take the first fish you catch; open its mouth
and you will find a four-drachma coin.
Take it and give it to them for my tax and yours."*
MATTHEW 17:27

Peter wanted Jesus to look good, so when the temple tax collectors asked if the Master paid the tax, Peter automatically said yes. He didn't realize that the Son of God really didn't have to pay tax to Himself. Yet to keep Peter's word, Jesus arranged payment for both of them.

Tax day probably wasn't the high point of most Jews' year, and April 15 may not be a high point for you, either. You might prefer giving to God than the government—and if you've been generous in your tithes and gifts, that may make a difference in how much Uncle Sam gets. But God doesn't say you shouldn't pay—even if you don't agree with everything your elected officials do with the money.

God can bless your money if you give it with the right attitude. Pray for the way it's used and the leaders who use it.

Lord, I want my taxes to go for good purposes. Guide the leaders who make use of them.

April 16

*"This poor widow has put more into
the treasury than all the others.
They all gave out of their wealth;
but she, out of her poverty, put in everything—
all she had to live on."*
MARK 12:43–44

Doesn't part of you wish you were as brave as the widow who dropped her last coins into the temple treasury? *How would I live if I gave that much?* you probably ask yourself. *What would I do?* Scary, isn't it?

Scripture doesn't tell us the widow went home to find money waiting for her. We can't guarantee that the story had that kind of happy ending.

But we know that, whatever happened, God knew what she had done and blessed her. Doesn't He promise to bless those who give?

Faith often means hanging on the edge, not knowing all the answers. Maybe for you it isn't putting your last pennies in the offering plate, but it's putting a tithe in when you don't know how you'll pay that last bill. Or maybe it's sharing the gospel with someone, when you don't know if he'll object.

That's life on the edge of faith.

Lord, I don't want to be so comfortable that I forget what life's like on the edge. Make my faith walk exciting.

April 17

*It is of the LORD'S mercies that we are not
consumed, because his compassions fail not.
They are new every morning:
great is thy faithfulness.*
LAMENTATIONS 3:22–23, KJV

Troubles seemed to overflow Craig. He spent
more and more time on the job as his boss loaded
him with work. His mom went into the hospital for
tests. His girlfriend disappeared from his life. The
pastor of his church resigned, and Craig wondered
if *anything* in life was stable. Troubles seemed to
eat Craig up inside.

Life's challenges can hit us hard—and suddenly.
One moment you have one problem you're dealing with, and the next you have three or four. *Has
God forgotten me? Will He leave me stranded?*
you may wonder.

Never. Compassion is God's "middle name."
Every day, even the lousy ones, He remains faith-
ful. You may not see the way He's working, but
He's out ahead, protecting you.

No trouble can eat you up when you belong to
God. It may nibble at your edges, but you won't be
consumed.

*Lord, faith isn't just emotions. When I get that empty,
stranded feeling, I know it's nothing You put in my
heart. I don't want to be eaten up with worry—just
consumed with Your Word.*

April 18

Thy word is a lamp unto my feet,
and a light unto my path.
I have sworn, and I will perform it,
that I will keep thy righteous judgments.
PSALM 119:105–106, KJV

Why should I read a book that's thousands of years old? What would those old guys know about modern life?"

If you haven't actually heard those words, you've heard that message from someone who doesn't value reading the Word.

The fact is, plenty of people, even those who've walked down a church aisle to commit themselves to Christ, have trouble spending time in the Bible.

But others pick up Scripture and new truths leap out at them, answering questions that have been on their hearts for a long time.

What's the difference?

Commitment. Spend regular time in the Word and seek out teaching in it, and the light goes on. Suddenly you begin to understand, and the Spirit comes alongside, teaching you new things.

At first you get out of the Word what you put into reading it. But as you get to know God better, that light burns brighter.

How's the light burning in your life?

Lord, when Your Word seems dry, keep me going.
I want to draw closer to You.

April 19

*It is God who arms me with strength
and makes my way perfect.*
2 Samuel 22:33

Trapped! You're on a plane, and you can't help but overhear that whining, complaining voice. *Could I climb out on the wing for a little quiet?* you wonder. You soon know all about the whiner, who tells more with that whine than words.

As a Christian, you're as public as that whiner. Everyone hears and sees all you do. But instead of griping, you exude kindness, gentleness, and sweetness. You make your fair share of mistakes, yet hecklers call you "Mr. Goody Two-shoes" or "Ms. Perfection" just to get a less-than-perfect reaction from you.

Any perfection doesn't stem from you, but from God. He's making you strong in Him. People see His righteousness, and it challenges them. Some react negatively.

But don't worry. If they don't like you, it's not *you* they're really seeing anyway—it's Jesus.

Jesus, whether or not they like it, I want others to see You in my life. Your perfection is better than anything I could offer.

April 20

You have not lied to men but to God.
ACTS 5:4

Okay, so maybe you aren't like Ananias. You've never lied about how much money you had to give. But are you honest with God?

That's tough. After all, to be totally honest with God might mean letting Him inside those deep, dark spaces that no one knows about. The date that was going so well, until. .·. Your real thoughts about that coworker. . . The way you *really* feel about things He's written in His Word. . .

We'd like to hide lots from God. Our messy lives just don't seem good enough for Him. The problem is, until we open up to Him, we'll never change. God doesn't barge into our hearts, ferreting out sin. Instead He woos us, shows us the right path, and invites us to give up those dark holes in our lives.

If we don't, we may not get suddenly wiped out, like Ananias, but a slow spiritual death creeps into our lives.

Is it creeping into *your* life?

Lord, it's hard to be honest with Someone as holy as You. But I want to be like You in this, too. Cleanse my heart.

April 21

Road rage starts as a minor incident—one car cuts off another, and at least one temper flares. If you drive on crowded roads, road rage may tempt you. You've had a rough day at work, but the first time someone cuts you off, it's no big thing. You remember you're God's child and hold back the anger. Several miles later, at the highway entrance, cars crowd you out. Finally you force your way into traffic, and a slow burn starts. The next guy who cuts you off triggers that anger.

You'd never track down the offender and destroy him. You just honk your horn or roll down the window and give him a piece of your mind. What's wrong with that?

No physical roadkill occurred, just spiritual roadkill. God doesn't tell us to get angry when we've had enough or when the day's been miserable. He tells us *never* to give in to anger.

Why add God's judgment to an already bad day?

Father, I want even my driving to reflect Your love. When I get behind the wheel, cover me with Your peace.

April 22

Remember those in prison
as if you were their fellow prisoners,
and those who are mistreated
as if you yourselves were suffering.
HEBREWS 13:3

It's not wrong to pray for people in prison for their crimes, but the author of Hebrews wasn't thinking of them when he wrote this. He was describing those imprisoned for their faith.

Did you know that more Christians have suffered for their faith in this century than in all the previous Christian centuries? That doesn't mean they've been teased for witnessing, excluded from one job because they wouldn't go with the flow, or felt peer pressure about mentioning the name of Jesus. They've been physically abused, lost their freedom, and even lost their lives.

Christians in the Sudan and China have faced such situations. Men and women in Arab nations have felt the pressure not to convert and faced persecution from their own families when they gave their hearts to Jesus.

You may never travel to those countries, but you can still reach them. Learn about persecution "hot spots"—where they are and what's going on. Then pray for Christians (and their persecutors). God crosses every political border.

Father, my heart breaks when I think of other believers suffering for You. Keep me faithful in prayer.

April 23

At the same time that my sanity was restored,
my honor and splendor were returned
to me for the glory of my kingdom. . . .
I was restored to my throne
and became even greater than before.
DANIEL 4:36

Nebuchadnezzar got so caught up in his own power as the king of Babylon that God humbled him. The king became like a wild animal. For seven years, he lost his sanity and became a wild man who ate grass.

At the end of those years, the proud ruler turned to God, and his sanity returned. Once Nebuchadnezzar recognized God's dominion, his kingdom was never the same. God restored all he had lost and much more—He made him even greater!

Like the king of Babylon, do you resist God, fearful that He'll overthrow your little kingdom and make you do everything you hate?

Then it's not Jesus you're thinking of.

God is a wonderful, generous Lord. Obey Him, and life's trials bring you better things, not destruction. He doesn't want to ruin your world, but to bless you beyond your expectations.

It's hard to believe You want me to have good things, Lord, when I focus on this world. Turn my eyes to You and give me a vision of Your blessing.

April 24

Those who cling to worthless idols
forfeit the grace that could be theirs.
JONAH 2:8

After three days and nights inside a fish tummy, Jonah doubtless felt as if God had given up on him. Separation from God's grace was painful. It hurt Jonah to know that his own misdeeds landed him in a stinky, wet, nasty fish belly. The only thing that kept the prophet disobedient was the thought, *If I do what God says, I might like what happens even less.*

Have you felt distance between you and God? Suddenly His grace seems far off, and your prayers go no farther than the ceiling, if that far.

If you're feeling apart from God, let that feeling remind you, just a bit, what it's like not to know Him. Take action to draw near Him again—confess sin, trust in Him, and obey His commands. But once you feel His grace, don't forget that He wants you to share it with others who feel trapped in a fish belly. Give His love away as freely as you received it.

Lord, it's such a blessing to draw close to You whenever I want. Help me share that blessing with others today.

April 25

*I will cut off. . .them that worship the host
of heaven upon the housetops.*
ZEPHANIAH 1:4–5, KJV

But the occult is dangerous," Brendan warned his church group. "Why—"

Another group member quickly cut him off, pooh-poohing his words. Some in the study did not want to admit that reading a horoscope was unbiblical.

Knowing Christ isn't a cheap guarantee that you can do anything you like and still spend eternity in heavenly bliss. Dabbling in astrology, palm reading, and Tarot cards isn't something God ignores in His people.

Zephaniah took the people of Judah to task for a similar divided allegiance. He never said that they didn't give God a piece of their lives. They did—but they held on to Baal worship, too. They looked to the stars for answers, as well as going to the temple.

God doesn't save a piece of your life, He saves all of it. A faithful response is to give Him your whole life in return. You can't do that if you're also trying to use occult methods to see what the future holds.

You may not know your whole future, but you know who holds it. Trust in Him.

Thank You, Lord, for holding my future. I want to trust You for everything.

April 26

*Praise be to the God and Father
of our Lord Jesus Christ,
the Father of compassion
and the God of all comfort.*
2 CORINTHIANS 1:3

"Lynn knew Matt and I just broke up and that I'm really hurting," Terri wailed to her roommate Dana. "Why would she come here to tell me that she and Wayne are getting married and then stay forever, talking about their plans?"

Dana tried to comfort Terri, explaining that Lynn had to share her joy. But Dana's heart went out to her roommate. Terri had been looking hopefully at bridal gowns just a month ago, expecting to plan a winter wedding.

When life hurts deeply, even well-meaning friends may not be able to reach our ache, and the slightest insensitivity on another's part can pain us to the core.

But Jesus reaches that place with a tender cure. He knows exactly how to heal our hurts. He won't say callous words that put a blade in our hearts. Instead He woos us with kindness and encourages us until we're heart-whole.

Reach for His gentle hand when you feel pain.

Lord, I know You can comfort me like no other. Help me turn to You when I hurt and offer Your comfort to others.

April 27

"Give us each day our daily bread."
LUKE 11:3

Getting caught up in a round of chores—laundry, cleaning, and shopping—isn't very exciting. But the work has to get done sometime, and even the worst housekeeper has to spend some time doing it.

Surely God can't have a purpose in this, we think. *There's nothing crucial to His kingdom here.*

Does God know you have to go to the cleaners, wash the car, and buy food? Of course He does. Our need for "daily bread"—and meat, and eggs, and even clean laundry—doesn't come as a surprise to Him. He provides for it all.

But in the midst of our busyness, we need to keep time for God. We can start the day with devotions, encourage a friend who phones just as we pick up a sponge to clean the bathroom, and reach out to someone in front of us in line at the grocery store.

Even dull days become exciting when you serve the Lord of the universe.

Lord, even days that don't seem to make great gains for Your kingdom are ordained by You. Help me touch others today.

April 28

You have planted much, but have harvested little.
You eat, but never have enough.
You drink, but never have your fill.
You put on clothes, but are not warm.
You earn wages, only to put them
in a purse with holes in it.
HAGGAI 1:6

S andy didn't have the best-paying job in the world, but she used her money carefully and could always pay her bills and give a tithe.

Her friend Alan rarely gave to the church, made twice as much money as Sandy, but never seemed to have a dollar in his pocket.

Some people reach the end of the month with their bills paid and their minds peaceful. Others always seem to need money, no matter how much they toss into their accounts.

You need to live below your income, spending less than you make. But no matter how much you make and how hard you try to keep a handle on it, if you don't give to God, there will be an empty hole in your pocket and a deeper one in your heart.

Obey Him, and somehow you'll have enough for all your needs.

Thank You, Father, for providing for all my needs. I want to give generously to You and do Your will today.

April 29

And the LORD shall be king over all the earth:
in that day shall there be one LORD,
and his name one.
ZECHARIAH 14:9, KJV

The name of Jesus used to grate against my nerves. Saying it was like squealing chalk against a blackboard," Alicia remembered. "I think, even before I knew Him, I couldn't get away from His authority."

There *is* something about the name of Jesus. Work in a factory, and you'll hear it uttered often, but not prayerfully. Yet who misuses the name of Allah, Buddha, or any other religious figure when things aren't going right? It's as if even people who don't believe in Jesus can't get away from His authority. Maybe they blame Him for anything that goes wrong, but they unknowingly recognize Him.

One day Jesus will return to rule the entire earth. Then, at His name, "every knee should bow" (Philippians 2:10). Christians will kneel willingly, glorifying the Risen One, but nonbelievers will be forced to acknowledge their Judge.

Today recognize Jesus for who He is. There's a lot of power, glory, and love in that name.

Lord, Your name is wonderful. I want the world to know it today.

April 30

Your fasting ends in quarreling and strife,
and in striking each other with wicked fists.
You cannot fast as you do today
and expect your voice to be heard on high.
Isaiah 58:4

People who fast have a real commitment to God. It takes a lot of faith to give up food.

But even an empty stomach becomes meaningless if it's done for outward show. Christians who fast and pray, yet live sinful lives, haven't drawn near God. What they're doing on the outside has nothing to do with what's on the inside, and their daily actions show that more clearly than a public fast.

Developing consistency in our spiritual lives is challenging. We can't act as if we're "in good" with God then fight with fellow Christians. We can't say one thing and do another.

Isaiah chided people who thought outward show was more important than heartfelt faith. In their pride they probably wondered why God didn't seem more receptive to their prayerful "suggestions" about how He should run the universe.

They weren't listening to God; they were trying to run the world. Are you?

Lord, I don't want to look good to others; I just want to know You, love You, and serve You with all my life. Keep me from pride.

May 1

Teach them the decrees and laws,
and show them the way to live
and the duties they are to perform.
EXODUS 18:20

Everyone new to a job needs to be taught what to do and how to do it. You have to ask some pretty stupid questions before you can even start your work. Even flipping a burger can be done in a number of ways, only one of which will be the "right" way. Then, once you get the procedures down pat, you'll go and violate some unwritten law that nobody ever mentioned. How are you supposed to learn all this stuff on your own?

You can't—at least not fast enough to avoid some serious goofs. You have to take notice of all these little things while you work, juggling everything at once. If you're fortunate, you'll find someone willing to give you some clues until you can handle it all alone. Treasure this kind soul. Then, when you're experienced and savvy, take a new hire under your wing and return the favor.

Lord, give me the patience I need to learn all the written and unwritten rules of my job. Give me one friend I can trust to fill me in, and I will do the same for another in the future.

May 2

*What? know ye not that your body is the temple
of the Holy Ghost which is in you,
which ye have of God?*
1 CORINTHIANS 6:19, KJV

How long has it been since you've seen a dentist? Have you had your eyes checked once since leaving home? Had your blood pressure taken lately?

Probably not. Once we're responsible for our own bodies, we tend to ignore them until something goes wrong. A throbbing tooth will get us to a dentist pretty fast, but we'll skip the six-month checkups until then. Of course, a regular checkup would have caught the tiny cavity that's now big enough to drive a truck through.

In the old days, when you paid for health care out of your own pocket, you might have had economic reasons for avoiding medical costs, but now most people are covered by health insurance. Use it. Regular checkups will save you a lot of problems later. You won't be twenty-something forever. Don't you want a mouth full of your own teeth when you hit fifty?

Father, remind me to take care of myself now, so I can enjoy good health later in life.

May 3

*And having food and raiment
let us be therewith content.*
1 TIMOTHY 6:8, KJV

What do you have for breakfast these days? A cup of coffee from 7-Eleven? Do you skip lunch and grab a candy bar? Is dinner hamburger and fries?

Most people who leave home to live on their own change their eating habits. Who has time to make a meat loaf or pot roast? Who knows how? It's a great feeling to be able to eat whatever and whenever you want, with no one prodding you to eat your vegetables.

But your body does have certain requirements and will tell you when it needs a shot of something green. When it does, listen to it. Find a good salad bar if you're not up to washing lettuce. Take a daily vitamin pill to be sure you're filling in the blanks in your diet. Find a fast-food place that serves "comfort food"—the food you were brought up on. Don't neglect your body's nutritional needs for too long, or it will begin to punish you.

Father, I believe my body is Your temple, and I need to take care of it. Show me how I can eat properly in the small amount of time I have available.

May 4

Do not be misled:
"Bad company corrupts good character."
1 CORINTHIANS 15:33

The world is full of "bad company" we can't avoid. The best we can do is recognize them for what they are and not let them influence our personal lives.

We do have a voice in whom we *choose* to hang around with, but it takes time to really know a person, so we make mistakes. We become friends with someone who is really fun to be with. He or she eases our loneliness, and then we discover that we really don't like some of the things going on. We want to break off the relationship, but that's hard. "Maybe it's not really all that serious." "Maybe I can change him."

It's at this point, when we begin rationalizing insupportable behavior, our good character becomes corrupted. We overlook one flaw after another until we can no longer say, "This is wrong. I can't do this." A person who can't see the difference between good and bad is a corrupt person.

Father, give me the wisdom to choose my friends carefully, and when I make a mistake, give me the courage to break off the relationship before I begin to think and act like a corrupt person myself.

May 5

*We must pay more careful attention,
therefore, to what we have heard,
so that we do not drift away.*
HEBREWS 2:1

All your life, Mom and Dad have taken responsibility for getting you to church, but that's over now. You may live miles from them or in the same town, but except for a little nagging, they can't control your actions anymore. It's on your head if you don't get yourself to church.

There are all kinds of excuses you can use, from not being able to find a friendly congregation to not feeling the need for church. It's easy to drift away, once your old habits have been broken and you're living in a new situation.

But Sunday's not the same without church. There's something nice missing from your week, even if you can't pinpoint it. Maybe Mom and Dad were right, and you need to pay more careful attention to what you have heard—from them and the Lord. Maybe it's time to find that friendly congregation and admit that you *need* to go to church.

Father, it's so easy to drift away from old habits, even the good ones. Help me remember the warmth of fellowship, the security of being part of a congregation, and my need for You.

May 6

For Christ's love compels us,
because we are convinced
that one died for all.
2 CORINTHIANS 5:14

Life pulls us in a lot of directions, and sometimes we forget a few old things so we can remember the new. We only have so much time, effort, and attention to spare.

But how can you forget love? Once you're on your own, you soon realize how scarce love of any kind really is. The world's a cold, unfriendly place when no one loves you.

Yet we all have unbounded love, if we want it. Christ loved us so much He died for us. Every single one of us can be a new person because of His love, and that love is just as available to you now as it was to those living nearly 2,000 years ago.

Maybe you could forget doctrine and prayers. Maybe you don't enjoy Bible study or the closeness of others in a congregation. Maybe you can live without hymns and ceremonies. But how can you forget love?

Father, thank You for Your love, which is always there when I need it. Others may not be faithful in their love for me, but You will never fail me.

May 7

Don't get involved in foolish, ignorant arguments that only start fights.
2 TIMOTHY 2:23, NLT

One of the first things an adult learns, usually the hard way, is to never argue about politics or religion. You probably had those arguments in high school and college, but that was different. You were young then, exploring your ideas.

As we get older, those ideas often turn to concrete. This happens to everyone; they have a set of core beliefs they want left alone, thank you very much, because it's the rock they stand on to keep their noses above the flood. You mess with it at your peril.

This doesn't mean you shouldn't witness. You have every right to express your beliefs and try to help others, but you have to be aware of the danger of bumping against someone's rock. The conversation will either die or become strident. The friendly banter, the give-and-take, will be over. Even if you haven't quite finished making all your points, it's time to back off, because you've gone past "conversation" and are nearing "foolish and stupid arguments."

Father, teach me to avoid arguments that can have no good ending for anyone and to respect the beliefs of others, even when I think they are wrong.

May 8

Remember now thy Creator in the days
of thy youth, while the evil days come not,
nor the years draw nigh, when thou shalt say,
I have no pleasure in them.
ECCLESIASTES 12:1, KJV

Right now is one of the best times of your life. You are young and strong, unafraid of the future, and eager to experience all that life will bring. Now is the time to remember your Creator and thank Him for everything He has given you. Now is the time to enjoy yourself, sing His praises, and keep His commandments.

Remember how you used to thank your mom when she gave you your favorite food for dinner or took you on a great vacation? You thanked her with your whole heart and happily obeyed her rules. The days she gave you Brussels sprouts, you undoubtedly did not thank her—or take the garbage out without complaining. It works the same way in your relationship with God. Now, while things are going well, be lavish in your thanks, because it will be harder to do as life gets harder.

Father, thank You for the joys of life I see all around me today. Teach me now, while I am still young, how to live in a way that pleases You.

May 9

May your father and mother be glad;
may she who gave you birth rejoice!
PROVERBS 23:25

What's a mother want on Mothers' Day? The least you can do is send a Mothers' Day card. Many mothers are grateful for just that. Just remember to sign it. Next up the ladder are flowers delivered by a florist. Next is a long phone call, even if it's collect. All are acceptable if you live more than two hours from home.

But if you really want to honor your mother, all you have to do is show up at home, with or without a card and some flowers. Or you can go crazy, personally take her out to dinner, and pay the bill.

It doesn't take much to please a mother. Then you can get back to your own life, knowing you gave her what she really wants—you.

Father, I know that whatever I do for my mother this day can never pay her back for everything she's done for me. If I can't be there for her today, help me find some other way to let her know I do think about her and still need her in my life.

May 10

By faith Abraham,
when called to go to a place he would
later receive as his inheritance,
obeyed and went, even though
he did not know where he was going.
HEBREWS 11:8

Life rarely turns out as you planned. Oh, you can sit down and list your life goals for the next five or ten years. This is actually a good idea, because it helps you focus on your priorities. Just don't be surprised when you look back five or ten years later and see how far off the mark you've strayed.

This doesn't mean you shouldn't plan. Some of the best things in your life will come to you because of planning. But some of the best things will also come without planning for them at all. That's what makes life so much fun. It's a daily surprise, and you need to stride into it with faith, even if you don't know where you're going.

Father, I know You will provide what's best for me, even if I don't understand at the time. Let me walk in faith, like Abraham, confident that You know my path better than I do.

May 11

*And others had trial of cruel mockings and
scourgings, yea, moreover of bonds and
imprisonment: They were stoned, they
were sawn asunder, were tempted, were slain
with the sword: they wandered about
in sheepskins and goatskins;
being destitute, afflicted, tormented;
(Of whom the world was not worthy).*
HEBREWS 11:36–38, KJV

Most of us will never have to face death for
our faith, but there are dangers in feeling too safe.
For one thing, someone in a safe country never
even thinks about martyrdom—*personal* martyrdom. We aren't prepared for it and have no idea
how we would react to that type of danger. What
would you do if you had to renounce your faith in
order to live? What would you do to keep your
children alive? You can't make these decisions
wisely and rationally when someone's pointing a
gun at your head, and there won't be any chance
to change your mind. Think about it now, while
there's time—just in case.

*Father, I don't even want to think about this hap-
pening to me, but give me the strength to do so and
the courage to do what I have to do, if the time
should ever come.*

May 12

She sets about her work vigorously;
her arms are strong for her tasks.
She sees that her trading is profitable,
and her lamp does not go out at night. . . .
Give her the reward she has earned, and
let her works bring her praise at the city gate.
PROVERBS 31:17–18, 31

Although this woman works herself to the bone, she's quite successful for her time, and the verse says she deserves to be praised at the city gate, which is where the village elders sat and governed.

No, society was not particularly good to women in those days, but it couldn't ignore this one, and it paid her the reward she had earned. That's about all anyone—male or female—can ask for today, too. Those who work hard and live righteous lives should be praised by the elders at the gate (or in the boardroom), whether they are men or women.

Lord, I can't begin to compare to this woman, who never seems to sleep, but I do work pretty hard, and I'd like a little recognition, too. When I have a really bad day and am feeling unappreciated, remind me that even when people don't appreciate me, I still have Your love.

May 13

Rise in the presence of the aged,
show respect for the elderly
and revere your God.
LEVITICUS 19:32

Parents have always taught basic manners: Cover your mouth when you cough, don't scratch in public, and so on, but lately manners have been ignored in our rush toward equality and self-expression. Life has become much less civil than it used to be.

We're not talking about how to tell a fish fork from a salad fork or the proper way to curtsey to royalty, neither of which has much to do with life today. We're talking about a general lack of respect for everyone, which leads to road rage, physical attacks on teachers, and other undesirable social acts.

Manners are not meaningless rules that only apply to the well-off. They are about well-earned respect and consideration for others. Think about the consequences of your act the next time you roll down your car window and prepare to show another driver what you think of him. Is this an act that is going to make the world a better place?

Father, my daily actions should be worthy of You. Help me show proper respect to all people, even when I'm upset and angry. Remind me of my manners and the great effect that even a simple thank you can have on the world.

May 14

*"Who of you by worrying can add
a single hour to his life?"*
MATTHEW 6:27

With a closet full of clothes, we worry about not having the right thing to wear. With a cupboard full of food, there's still nothing to eat. These are minor worries not based on fact, but they continue to nag at us until we go out and buy the "right" clothes or cram the cupboard with enough food to feed a small nation.

Many people have more legitimate worries—actual needs that consume every waking moment in a struggle for survival. What's amazing is that many of these people are still happy, despite their problems. How do they do it? Perhaps they've read a little farther in Matthew 6, where Jesus promised, "Seek first his kingdom and his righteousness, and all these things will be given to you as well" (v. 33).

Worry wastes time because it produces nothing, while seeking God and His kingdom is always a worthwhile activity that will banish trivial worries and provide us with whatever we need.

Father, I know the rent money will be there when I need it if I concentrate on living righteously and don't let my worries paralyze me. Times may get tough, but I can make it with Your help.

May 15

For, lo, the winter is past, the rain is over and
gone; The flowers appear on the earth;
the time of the singing of birds is come,
and the voice of the turtle is heard in our land.
SONG OF SOLOMON 2:11–12, KJV

Even the hardest winter eventually gives way to spring, and signs of new life surround us. And yet nature has become irrelevant to many of us who live and work in a climate-controlled life. The closest most of us get to nature is when we're splashed by a taxi or the buses are thrown off schedule by snow and we're late for work. Nature is mostly a matter of inconvenience to us.

And yet nothing can make us feel as fully human as nature, if we get out there and really experience it. Spend some time out there and your whole outlook on life can change. Nature has no patience with self-involved humans. It humbles us, sometimes it hurts us, but it also teaches us that God is pleased with *all* His creations, and we are only one of them.

Lord, sometimes I forget about the breadth of Your creation and feel I am the only one who counts. Give me the opportunity to become more involved with all of Your creation, so I can see myself in perspective.

May 16

Do not forget to entertain strangers,
for by so doing some people have entertained
angels without knowing it.
HEBREWS 13:2

In biblical times—and today, in many parts of the world—anyone who came to the door was given food and drink for the journey. The next house or town was often far away, and entertaining strangers could save their lives.

This isn't something we feel safe doing today. We don't even open the door to strangers, let alone entertain them. So how are we supposed to keep this command?

One way is to join a group effort, such as working at a food bank or soup kitchen. Doing volunteer work at a nursing home or hospital is another option, as is driving for Meals on Wheels.

There are also individual ways to help, little acts of kindness. You can check up on elderly neighbors once in a while, perhaps offering to run errands or drive them to a doctor's appointment. You can give way to another driver or step out of line at the supermarket and allow someone to go ahead of you. None of these actions puts you in danger, but they are all forms of entertaining strangers.

Father, show me how I can be helpful to others in little ways that count.

May 17

And if ye call on the Father, who without respect of persons judgeth according to every man's work, pass the time of your sojourning here in fear.
1 PETER 1:17, KJV

The world thinks in the present tense. Christians tend to think in the future tense, with a good understanding of the past. Like anyone else, they want to be successful, but they knows God's will for their lives is more important. They are willing to give up a lot to lead righteous lives, knowing their rewards may be far in the future. They praise God for all His blessings in good times and in bad. Christians start with God and work down to themselves.

Anyone who thinks in such a totally different way is bound to be a stranger here, not quite at home in this world. A far better world awaits Christians, the place they can truly call home. Living as strangers is not easy, but it's the only way that makes any sense.

Lord, thank You for the salvation that is mine for the asking. If it causes me to feel like a stranger here, remind me that my home is with You.

May 18

But if a widow has children or grandchildren,
these should learn first of all to put
their religion into practice by caring for
their own family and so repaying
their parents and grandparents,
for this is pleasing to God.
1 TIMOTHY 5:4

Before you know it, your parents will be old. You probably won't notice it as it happens, but one day you'll see your mother rubbing her sore back or hear your father groan as he stands, and it will suddenly hit you that they aren't the parents of your youth anymore. In time, you'll find yourself faced with having to parent your own parents. It's scary, unnatural, and lonesome.

How do you prepare yourself for this time? The best way is to keep in touch with your parents now. Find out how they feel about medical care and retirement. What do they want their old age to be like, and what don't they want? Are they afraid of outliving their savings, or are they financially secure?

Of course, this requires tact on your part, but now is the time to learn who your parents really are.

Father, I hate watching my parents grow old. Give me all the patience and love I'll need to make their later years as happy and full as possible.

May 19

He is the Rock, his work is perfect:
for all his ways are judgment: a God of truth and
without iniquity, just and right is he.
DEUTERONOMY 32:4, KJV

For centuries, wise men and women have had a hard time with this verse, so it's not unusual for the average person to ask the obvious question: If God is just, why isn't His world? Why don't the good prosper and the evil fail? Why do starvation and genocide still rage today?

One obvious answer is that God is working with flawed materials—us. Over the course of history, we've changed the world, not always for the better. He gave us dominion over the earth, and our sin has corrupted a perfectly just situation, which does not change the fact that God Himself is still what He has always been.

Maybe the best answer to the just-God/unjust-world problem is to admit that we don't know what's going on. We're simply not seeing the whole picture. Even if we could, we probably wouldn't understand it. Some things you just have to take on faith. God is still in the world, doing what only He can do.

Father, I place my life in Your hands, certain that all things work according to Your will, whether I understand or not.

May 20

God has not left us alone on the earth to struggle through our lives without guidance. Whether we call it God's voice or our own conscience, it is there, and it does help. We also have the freedom to ignore the voice and go our own way. There are no strings attached to us that God can pull to keep us on the path. He will tell us which way to go, but we control our own legs.

The same thing happens to parents who raise their children properly and then can do nothing but watch when something goes wrong and their children turn to drugs or crime. Imagine the pain those parents feel and then multiply it to infinity and you will only begin to understand a fraction of the pain we must cause our heavenly Father.

Don't let the world's uproar drown out the voice you hear behind you. It's the best friend you will ever have.

Father, I want to follow Your path. Help me listen when You guide me in the way I should go.

May 21

*Ye are all the children of light,
and the children of the day:
we are not of the night,
nor of darkness.*
1 Thessalonians 5:5, kjv

There's nothing wrong with the night in itself. It's a time of peace and rest and relaxation, which we all need. A child of the light—a Christian—can enjoy both day and night.

Yet there is something about the night that worries us. Not many horror movies are filmed in bright daylight, and echoing footsteps behind us in the night can raise the hairs on the back of our neck. There's a sense of danger in the night that we can never completely escape. Maybe that's part of its attraction.

The trick is to be able to enjoy the night without taking it into our souls and becoming part of it. As Christians, we have seen the light and know wrong from right. We shouldn't do anything in the dark that we wouldn't do in the sunshine. We cannot *belong to* the night, because we belong to Jesus.

Lord, You bring sunshine into my life where once there was darkness. Thank You for Your love and protection at all hours of the day and night.

May 22

But now they mock me,
men younger than I,
whose fathers I would have
disdained to put with my sheep dogs.
JOB 30:1

Job had fallen on hard times, and the young men who once looked up to him for wisdom and advice now scorned him and spit in his face, not showing a shred of respect for someone older. In the end, however, God restored Job to twice his prior rank and power, and we can be sure the disrespectful young men soon wished they'd kept their mouths shut.

Being discreet is always wise. People in power do fall, but a good number of them climb back, too. If your supervisor at work seems to be in trouble with the powers that be, don't make the mistake of publicly turning on him or failing to show him the respect his position deserves. If you're secretly happy to see him in trouble, keep your feelings a secret. Otherwise, you not only show disrespect for one unfortunate person, you also show disrespect for his office, and people will remember what you said and how you acted.

Father, teach me how to show the proper respect for those above me, no matter what the current situation may be.

May 23

Young man, it's wonderful to be young!
Enjoy every minute of it.
ECCLESIASTES 11:9, NLT

This verse ends, "but know that for all these things God will bring you to judgment" (NIV). Doesn't the ending of this verse contradict the beginning? Wouldn't it make more sense to forego the happiness to be safe during the judgment?

No, it would be foolish to live that way. A Christian should enjoy life, and youth is the time to enjoy it to its fullest. A good person does not have to walk around avoiding all fun just to be safe. Those who do so lead lonely, unfulfilling lives, which is certainly not what God had in mind for the faithful.

What this verse is saying is that there are some limits you'll have to be aware of while you're having fun. Some activities are inappropriate for the faithful. But you know that, and you know it's perfectly possible to enjoy living the faithful life. Don't wrap yourself up in "thou shalt nots" and deny yourself all the fun God means you to enjoy.

Father, show me the limits I need to know, but help me lead a happy, fulfilling life at the same time, a good witness of Your love.

May 24

Set up road signs; put up guideposts.
Take note of the highway,
the road that you take.
JEREMIAH 31:21

We all have to see the path we're walking, or we'll end up in the bushes, not where we thought we were going. Life's a pretty long road, so putting up a few mental road signs is a good idea. When you hit a crossroads, get out your ethical road map and choose your path deliberately. You'll either decide, "No, I don't want to go there," or, "Yes, this is the way."

Note that this is *your* road map; we each have to draw our own. You can give advice to other travelers you meet along the way, but you can't force them to follow your path. In the same way, you can't blindly follow some other traveler, hoping she's going where you want to go. If she suddenly veers off on a side road you don't know, you'll never find your way back to the right path. Be aware of your decisions and follow the way you know is right.

Father, there are so many choices I have to make in my life, and I can't see where they lead in the end. Give me Your guidance so I will end up next to You.

May 25

*"Whoever can be trusted with very little
can also be trusted with much,
and whoever is dishonest with very little
will also be dishonest with much."*
LUKE 16:10

You're just starting off in your job, and nobody trusts you with very much. You do what you're told, day after day, and it gets pretty boring after a while. Where's the challenge? What do you have to do before you get to make a few decisions or enjoy some responsibility?

Unfortunately, you have to keep on doing just what you're doing now—only better. You have to master the boring stuff first, really get it down pat, and be the best "nobody" anyone's ever seen. Don't think no one's watching, because they are. Even boring work has to be done well, and if you sleep-walk through the day, it will be noticed. But if you prove yourself trustworthy in this job, a better one will be ahead for you. At the very least, you'll end up with a good reference for your resume.

Father, when my work gets so boring I want to nod off about midafternoon, remind me that I hold the keys to my own success in my own hands. I may be a nobody now, but I won't be for long, with Your help.

May 26

These commandments that I give you today
are to be upon your hearts.
Impress them on your children.
Talk about them when you sit at home
and when you walk along the road,
when you lie down and when you get up.
DEUTERONOMY 6:6–7

Moses was trying to impress on the Israelites the importance of following God's commandments to the letter. They were constantly to keep God's laws in mind and teach them to their children, from generation to generation. The problem was, Moses wasn't going with them to the Promised Land, and time has a way of blurring memories, especially when you've gotten what you want. Nothing makes you forget the past as fast as success, and soon enough the Israelites would disregard the rules, despite all God and Moses had done for them.

We do the same thing now. We get in trouble and beg for help, swearing everlasting devotion. "I'll do anything You ask, I promise!" Once we're safe, we forget our promises.

You're human, and you will sometimes fail, but a promise is still a promise.

Lord, often I promise something I can't deliver. Make me more faithful in honoring my word, so I can be a good example and glorify You by my actions.

May 27

The last time God really lost His temper, He killed off everyone in the world except Noah and his family and a representative sample of every animal that filled the world. God must have known that humans can't live with a threat like that hanging over their heads, and He promised that sort of mass punishment was a thing of the past. Humanity itself was safe, even though individuals still had to deal with individual judgment. God promised to differentiate between individuals and humanity as a whole.

Besides taking a load of fear off our backs, this promise also serves as an example of how we should deal with our own anger. We have to differentiate, too. Just because a bald man fired you doesn't mean all bald men are to be hated. You can't hate all women when one breaks your heart. You don't kick all dogs after one bites your leg. If God, in His righteous anger, promises not to punish by category, can we do anything less?

Father, thank You for judging fairly, no matter how we displease You with our actions. Teach me to do the same.

May 28

God places the lonely in families.
PSALM 68:6, NLT

It's kind of hard to be lonely in the midst of a family. Someone's always sitting at the kitchen table, waiting for you to get off the phone, or banging on the bathroom door. Eventually you move out, get your own place, and rule your own roost. It's wonderful for a while. You do what you want, eat what you want, and leave your clothes where you want.

But soon the silence gets to you. You start leaving the television on, just for the company. You sing along with the commercials. You call home just to hear your sisters fighting in the kitchen. You begin the frightening process of dating, at first just for the company. If you're fortunate, you find the right person and—bingo—you have your *own* family.

Loneliness has its purpose. It forces most of us to relate to others in meaningful ways, to build families of one sort or another. Loneliness's ultimate success is its own defeat.

Lord, sometimes I get so lonely I can't stand it. Help me find the family I need, whether it's a group of close friends from work, a circle of people from church, or a husband or wife.

May 29

The wicked man flees though no one pursues,
but the righteous are as bold as a lion.
PROVERBS 28:1

We all know people who are constantly on the run, trying to escape something only they can see. They seem determined to self-destruct. Some men are perfectly happy dating until their dates say, "I love you" and send them into panicked retreats. Others do remarkably well at work, only to sabotage their own success as if they were afraid of it. For some reason, they feel unworthy of anything good that comes their way.

Generally people who act this way are not wicked. Something in their backgrounds makes them feel inferior, and escape is their way of dealing with unaccustomed success.

Unfortunately, the same response is also found in those who have good reasons for feeling guilty and threatened. Sometimes it's hard to distinguish between the truly guilty and those who flee for psychological reasons. Neither is easy to live or work with, but we have to be careful not to apply the term *wicked* to those who do not deserve it.

Lord, give me discernment and keep me from misjudging people I may not fully understand. I expect to be given the benefit of the doubt and need to do the same for others.

May 30

A quick-tempered man does foolish things.
PROVERBS 14:17

People handle anger in various ways. Some manage to push it down and continue as if they never felt it (probably giving themselves ulcers in the process). Others kick chairs in private but soon come to terms with their anger. Still others blow up and immediately feel better. We tend to react to anger the same way our parents did, for better or for worse.

In the same way, we all have different boiling points. It takes a lot to get some people angry, while others erupt at the slightest provocation.

However you react to anger, you need to maintain control. Anger makes us stupid. We do and say things we would never do under normal circumstances, starting fistfights or saying words we can never take back.

When anger takes over, we need to get away if we can't control ourselves. Go hide out in the rest room, if necessary. Shut a door behind you until you are back in control. A real man does not hit. A strong woman asserts control over herself, not over others.

Father, when I want to strike out in anger, whether verbally or physically, give me the self-control I need to avoid doing anything stupid.

May 31

Go from the presence of a foolish man, when thou perceivest not in him the lips of knowledge.
PROVERBS 14:7, KJV

A lot of foolish people are fun to be with. They tend to be the life of the party, always a little wild and irresponsible, doing things we would never dream of doing and collecting followers like a magnet collects paper clips. Some of them are good people and loyal friends, too. They're a little stupid at times, but harmless.

Most of them, however, you wouldn't trust for good advice, for the serious decisions we all have to make. For that, we seek out someone a little more mature and probably a lot more boring, people who actually have a serious side. You can ask advice of the life of the party, but you have to take what he says with a grain of salt, never sure if he's being serious or just pulling your leg.

Father, help me choose my advisors carefully and not be pulled in by charm when what I need is a carefully thought-out response.

June 1

*The man said, "This is now bone
of my bones and flesh of my flesh;
she shall be called 'woman,'
for she was taken out of man."*
GENESIS 2:23

Warm sunny June brings out the brides and grooms in a flurry. After they graduate, couples who want to spend their lives together face a decision-making time. *Is this the person God has for me?* each has to ask.

If you've decided to marry this June, it doesn't matter if your day is a sunshiny blue one or the buckets-of-rain sort. Though good weather may make travel easy for your guests, it isn't the most important thing about getting married. Neither is the size of your reception or the clothes you wear.

When two people unite in marriage, they're symbolizing a deeper unity. Instead of making two out of one, as with Adam and Eve, God makes one out of two. They're meant to be bound together for life.

Living out that commitment every day is more important than weather, the number of guests, or clothes. Those things last in your memory, but they can't replace a lifetime together.

Lord, thank You for reminding me of the importance of marriage. I want to make mine one that lasts a lifetime.

June 2

*Do not rebuke an older man harshly,
but exhort him as if he were your father.*
1 TIMOTHY 5:1

That older guy makes you nuts! All you hear from him is the things you can't do, to the point where you wonder if you'll ever be old enough to walk a dog.

Some terrific people twenty, thirty, and even forty years older than you have positive outlooks and encourage you in most things you take on. They're joyful people, and you're glad to be around them.

But that one person. . .

When your personal naysayer starts carping, your mind lists all the ways you'd like to respond. *I'm not a baby anymore, I have a place of my own. You know, my boss trusts me more than you do.* Hold on—long enough to toss those words out of your mind. Exploding won't improve your situation. He'll just go away thinking he was right after all. Instead, prove your maturity by treating him gently.

Timothy was a young pastor trying to lead older folks. Some didn't want to listen, so Paul advised him to talk to the older generation, not blow up.

Take Paul's advice, and they'll eventually respect you.

When others doubt my maturity, Lord, help me curb my anger and answer with love.

June 3

These men are blemishes at your love feasts, eating with you without the slightest qualm— shepherds who feed only themselves.
JUDE 12

Godless men had slipped into the church, misleading the brethren, seducing them to believe they could continue to sin and never receive God's correction. Jude called these false teachers "shepherds who feed only themselves."

Can you imagine a shepherd sitting on a barren hill, hungry animals all around him, enjoying his lunch? The baas and bleating would almost deafen him. He'd have to care for them.

Unlike sheep, people who fall in with wrong teaching rarely recognize the emptiness of what they're taking in. Instead, they keep following, filling their stomachs with useless calories of spiritual junk food, never understanding that they're barely being fed at all.

Don't follow false teachers. They're here today, gone tomorrow. Nothing they do can last, because they aren't founded on the bedrock of God's Word.

Lord, I don't want to be a wrong teacher any more than I want to follow one. Make my words reflect Your truth, and help my ears discern anything that doesn't reflect You.

June 4

God is jealous, and the LORD revengeth;
the LORD revengeth, and is furious;
the LORD will take vengeance on his adversaries,
and he reserveth wrath for his enemies.
NAHUM 1:2, KJV

Plenty of folks are perfectly willing to accept a wimpy kind of god—a perfectly inoffensive, powerless being who never interferes with their lives, never does anything *they* don't agree with, and *never* gets angry. This isn't God. Instead they've packed their own thinking in a little plastic doll, an idol created in their own image.

Imagine the anger any father would feel at having his son slighted! Well, God isn't just any father. He gave a unique Son. The perfect Man died to save sinners. To cost your Son such pain and then receive the message "Don't interfere with my life" from sinners deserves an angry response. Justice wouldn't be done if God acted otherwise.

No idol shows anger, but God is no wimp. If people won't accept the most precious gift God had to give, they can pay for it themselves—with their own lives.

What will your life cost?

Father God, though I deserved wrath, You sent Your Son for me. I don't want to ignore His sacrifice.

June 5

How long, O LORD, must I call for help,
but you do not listen?
Or cry out to you, "Violence!"
but you do not save?
HABAKKUK 1:2

We'd like to think believers never suffer serious, long-term wrongs. All Christians' troubles should be minor ones; after all, don't we serve God?

When we think this way, we've created a God who's almost at our beck and call. We're acting as if we're favored ones to whom He caters.

God didn't save us to place us in an ivory tower, apart from the miseries of this world. He didn't do that to Jesus, and He won't do it for us. Anyone who's been a Christian for long can tell you we don't always get instant prayer answers. Like Habakkuk, we'll find our faith tested by a long wait.

But at the end of God's delays, He often does something greater than anything we expected. Though His response may take days, weeks, or years, it comes at the right time.

Don't limit His work in your life by failing to pray.

Jesus, You're Lord of my life, not my personal slave. Help me to seek Your will in prayer.

June 6

*The LORD God is my strength, and he will make
my feet like hinds' feet, and he will make me
to walk upon mine high places.*
HABAKKUK 3:19, KJV

Habakkuk had a hard time understanding God
—Israel was a mess, and the Lord didn't seem to do
anything about it. So the prophet went straight to
the source to lodge his complaints—God Himself.

After a long conversation with Him, Habakkuk
still didn't understand everything God was doing.
The prophet didn't have all the answers, but he'd
developed trust in God's sovereignty. The Creator
was in control, and the prophet had faith again.

Even when you can't understand everything
God is working out in your life, can you praise
Him as sovereign Lord? Can you be confident in
Him and climb to the mountaintop of belief?

If not, go to Him in prayer. Share your doubts
and concerns, and give Him your burdens. Like
Habakkuk, in a short while praise will overflow
your heart.

*Understanding all You do, Lord, is impossible. But
I still trust that You are faithful. What I can't understand here, You can show me in heaven.*

June 7

*Then I said to them, "You see the trouble
we are in: Jerusalem lies in ruins,
and its gates have been burned with fire.
Come, let us rebuild the wall of Jerusalem,
and we will no longer be in disgrace."*
NEHEMIAH 2:17

O vercome with discouragement, the Jews who had returned to Jerusalem from exile huddled in a city open to invaders. Broken walls surrounded what was left of the city, and even its gates were burned. But no one started a citywide rebuilding project.

When Nehemiah heard of the situation, instead of hunkering down in fear, he got permission to rebuild the walls. He traveled to Jerusalem, inspected the site, and confronted the people. Encouragement and a plan were all the people needed—Nehemiah gave them both.

Sometimes every Christian needs lifting up. When job hunting gets you down, it's great to have someone show you the ropes and say something heartening. If you're struggling with sin, a seasoned Christian can share how she overcame the same temptation.

Don't let discouragement get the best of you. Reach out for help!

When I feel lower than a snake's navel, Lord, it's hard to tell others. Help me reach out for help.

June 8

Therefore we are buried with him by baptism into death: that like as Christ was raised up from the dead by the glory of the Father, even so we also should walk in newness of life.
ROMANS 6:4, KJV

You've been a Christian for a while, and that brand-new, clean feeling that came with a new faith has slowly evaporated.

Maybe, you ponder, *new is only for baby Christians. I know I've made "progress,"* you encourage yourself. *I'm not the same person I was before I knew Jesus.* But something's missing.

God didn't make Jesus new for a day, week, or month, and then let Him get "old" again. He eternally raised Him from the dead, so through baptism we can share His new life forever.

If vibrant faith has left you, some "old" things probably tarnish your new life. Legalistic or critical attitudes, disobedience, and doubt take the shine off a once-new faith, until you barely know you've been washed in the Lamb's blood.

But repentance during a let's-clear-the-air time with God returns the "new" to eternal life.

Spend time with Him in prayer.

Empty me of old things that keep me apart from You, Lord. I want to spend every new day close by Your side.

June 9

I revealed myself to those who did not ask for me; I was found by those who did not seek me. To a nation that did not call on my name, I said, "Here am I, here am I."
ISAIAH 65:1

The emptiness in her heart didn't even have a name when Jesus began to reach out to Janice. All she knew was a restlessness inside that nothing seemed to fill—not friends, good times, or New Age philosophies, though she'd tried to find peace in each. Caught in a narrow alley of confusion, Janice didn't know where to turn when Gail met her and introduced her to Jesus.

No matter how huge the emptiness in our hearts, we don't suddenly wake up one morning and say, "Jesus, that's the answer!" unless God has worked in our lives. Sin so mars our thinking that we can't begin to understand our own need. But God knows it. Despite our disobedience, He calls us anyway.

He hasn't stopped calling us, either. When life blindsides us, we feel that touch and hear His voice, reminding us that now we're His people—those He came to save.

Thank You, that when I wasn't even worth saving, Lord, You touched my life and made me whole.

June 10

*We did not follow cleverly invented stories
when we told you about the power and
coming of our Lord Jesus Christ,
but we were eyewitnesses of his majesty.*
2 PETER 1:16

Have you been in a courtroom and heard witnesses describe the same accident? Each sees something different. Though they were all there, each person's story varies. By careful listening, jurors come to a conclusion about just what went on. If parts of the story don't seem to agree, jurors have to decide which witness had the best knowledge.

The Bible consists of eyewitness accounts, too. The writers saw God's majesty and testified to it. They wrote across thousands of years, from various situations. Yet their stories all agree in amazing detail. When one seems different, it's an eyewitness report from another viewpoint, but all the stories meet together to form a glorious whole.

Sixty-six books that agree! How unlikely in the world of human beings. How certain when God's the author.

Lord, how wonderful is Your Word. Thank You for sharing it with me.

June 11

"Ye are my friends,
if ye do whatsoever I command you."
JOHN 15:14, KJV

Tina had more than her share of weddings in her future. Just after graduation, two friends were getting married. A week later, a cousin planned to say her vows, with Tina as maid of honor. By the end of June, Tina decided, her pockets would be empty.

But it wasn't the financial strain that bothered Tina. Her at-a-standstill romantic life was the real problem.

Three weddings, she thought, *and not a date for one of them.*

Tina wanted to share her friends' happiness, but being odd girl out hurt. It wouldn't have been so bad if there hadn't been *so many* weddings when she wasn't dating anyone.

Without even asking, Tina knew what Jesus wanted her to do. Shelving her own hurts, she went to the weddings and rejoiced in her friends' blessings. To her surprise, she had a great time and made a few new friends just because she didn't have a date!

Friendship with Jesus doesn't mean you'll always have a date—it means you'll always have a Friend.

When it's hard to obey Your commands, remind me, Friend, that I need to stick with You through the fun times and the tough ones.

June 12

I have set before you life and death,
blessing and cursing: therefore choose life,
that both thou and thy seed may live:
That thou mayest love the LORD thy God,
and that thou mayest obey his voice,
and that thou mayest cleave unto him.
DEUTERONOMY 30:19–20, KJV

You're moving into a new life. As you graduate, a whole world sits out there to discover.

But it's a *big* world. Looking at the decisions you'll face and the things that could go wrong, you may feel scared.

Life's made up of a lot of decisions—do I move here, take that job, go along with the program or break away from it? More important, life is made up of moral choices that have even more impact on your future.

Bad moral choices can spell death for relationships, but good ones bring them new life. Choices close opportunities to you (after all, who wants to hire a thief?) or open up new vistas.

If you're really into the Word, you know what those right choices are. They're all in the Book. Put them to work in your life, and you'll be blessed!

When I read Your Word, I see the things I should do. Give me strength, Lord, to follow through with right choices.

June 13

The fool says in his heart, "There is no God."
They are corrupt, their deeds are vile;
there is no one who does good.
PSALM 14:1

When God calls someone a fool, He's very serious. In Scripture, fools are those who don't believe in Him.

We may call ourselves a fool when we spill milk or forget to pick something up at the store. We should have known better, but we just weren't paying attention. Yet this sort of carelessness isn't the kind of foolishness God talks about in His Word.

To God, anyone who ignores the obvious messages He's given the world is missing more than mental focus. Real foolish thinking—such as self-centeredness and disregard for right—steeps a person in wickedness. Apart from God, no one does good.

We don't need to be hard on ourselves when we forget to pick up bread at the grocery store, but we do need to be careful that we don't emulate the works of the truly foolish—those who don't believe God even exists.

Lord, any goodness I do comes from You. When others deny You, I want to stand firm in faith instead of acting as if You don't exist.

June 14

"The Lord bless him!"
Naomi said to her daughter-in-law.
"He has not stopped showing
his kindness to the living and the dead. . . .
That man is. . .one of our kinsman-redeemers."
RUTH 2:20

The Old Testament world didn't offer women great career paths. Once their husbands died, as with Ruth and Naomi, they could find themselves barely able to live.

So God developed a way to take care of widows and orphans: The nearest male relative was to marry a widow and care for the family. Not the most romantic marriage proposal, you might think, but the truth God was showing here was more than hearts and flowers. He had a spiritual lesson in mind.

Until we know Jesus, we're all like a widow. Spiritual poverty binds us tightly, and we can't unwrap it from our souls. So we need a rescuer—someone who will come close to us and pay a price.

No earthly relative can do that for us, but our Brother Jesus can. He redeems us from our spiritual poverty and gives us a new life. Like Naomi, we suddenly find a life that seemed blighted and hopeless is bright with promise.

Sometimes, Jesus, I'm blind to my own spiritual poverty. Thank You for becoming my Kinsman-redeemer and buying me out of sin.

June 15

*Worship the Lord with gladness;
come before him with joyful songs.*
PSALM 100:2

Some music sounds good to you—and some is just an irritating noise. But you've probably found that your "noise" is another person's "sounds good."

Church music is part of the "noise" vs. "sounds good" debate. If your congregation likes the "oldies and moldies" of Christian music and you like the latest tunes on the Christian music shelves, you may be tempted to hold your ears during services.

Chances are the music you can't stand is favored by your pastor or music leader. Maybe other church members have encouraged the music director to play it. Asking anyone to change it could start World War III.

This psalm doesn't mention the kind of music churches should play—it doesn't specify classical, pop, rock music, or even Old Testament-style music. That's because the music isn't important—worshipping God is. He deserves our praise, no matter what the song is. A joyful heart can always praise Him.

Whether or not your church is tuned in to your music style, sing with all your heart.

Lord, I want to praise You, not start a war. Thank You for music I enjoy. Let me sing Your praises today.

June 16

Jana sat in the crowded doctor's office, miserable with a head cold and barely paying attention to her surroundings. If only she could get in to see the doctor and get home and to bed!

She barely noticed the grimacing man across from her, until another patient told the nurse, "He's in more pain than I am, please take him first."

Jana admired the woman, but guilt stabbed her heart. *I never realized he was in such pain,* she thought. *If I had, would I have done the same, even though it meant a longer wait?*

Doing good for others—especially those outside our circle of friends—means tuning in to their needs. Do we block ourselves behind a pseudo-spiritual wall and a "don't touch" mentality? Or do we open up to others, talk to hurting people, and offer them Jesus' help?

After all, that's only a small part of what He gave us.

Jesus, reaching out is hard when I get boxed into myself. Open my heart and eyes, so I can help others.

June 17

*May I never boast except in
the cross of our Lord Jesus Christ,
through which the world has been crucified
to me, and I to the world.*
GALATIANS 6:14

Stacie went to a great church. She was growing in Christ as she never had before. When she and other members of her church visited other churches, they always mentioned that theirs was the best church around.

One day Stacie's friend Paul, who went to another church, shocked her by asking if she was more attached to her church than to Jesus: "It seems you think your church can never be wrong and that every church should be just like it."

At first she was mad, but later Stacie caught Paul's drift. Nothing should be more important than the Savior in her life. Though they went to different churches, she and Paul were brother and sister in Christ. If she acted as if going to her church was more important than knowing Jesus, she was out of line spiritually.

Support your church, think well of it, but realize that God works through other congregations, too. Keep your eyes on Jesus, and you won't go wrong.

Lord, I don't want churchgoing to get in the way of my faith. Build me up in You, not in a building or way of worship.

June 18

And the frogs died out of the houses,
out of the villages, and out of the fields.
And they gathered them together upon heaps:
and the land stank.
EXODUS 8:13–14, KJV

Pharaoh's sin stank in God's nose. So to let the ruler of Egypt know what it was like, God covered his land with dead, smelly frogs. No one in Egypt could get away from the putrid results of their ruler's disobedience. You might say it smelled to high heaven.

All Pharaoh had to do to end the plagues was let the Hebrew people go, but Egypt's ruler couldn't get the picture. Stuck in sin, he couldn't face the loss of his slaves. He backed out on his promise every time. The powerful ruler was the *real* slave.

When we're caught in sin, our wrongdoing reeks. God may not litter our houses with frogs, but somehow He lets us know. Take the Christian who complains constantly about the wrongs others do him and alienates all his friends. Because loneliness stinks, he'll start to listen to God and stop complaining.

Has your life gotten pretty stinky lately? Clean out the sin and breathe in fresh air.

Thank You, Jesus, for cleansing the sin from my life. Scour the filthy corners of my life, so Your Spirit can freshen my soul.

June 19

*My intercessor is my friend as
my eyes pour out tears to God;
on behalf of a man he pleads with God
as a man pleads for his friend.*
JOB 16:20–21

How do you pray for others? Is it merely, "Bless John, bless Jane"? Imagine yourself in God's shoes, listening to such a shopping list of prayer. Pretty boring, isn't it?

Hearing such stuff must be harder for Him than praying it is for us. God's heart breaks when He thinks of all the blessings we could ask for that He would gladly give. But if He gave what we asked, what would that be? Are we looking for healing, peaceful relationships, conversion, or a thousand other things?

We'll never quite know how prayer works to move God's hand. But through the Spirit, who intercedes for us, we can bring the needs of friends, family, and even Christians who live half a world away to the Father. Lives begin to change, and we can praise God for His works.

The Spirit intercedes for you every day. Are you interceding for others, too?

Father God, fill me with Your love for others. Let my prayer time be a blessing to the world.

June 20

And Joseph's ten brethren went down to buy corn in Egypt. But Benjamin, Joseph's brother, Jacob sent not with his brethen; for he said, "Lest peradventure mischief befall him."
GENESIS 42:3–4, KJV

Jacob might never have learned what happened the day Joseph disappeared, but he undoubtedly had some suspicions. Hadn't the favorite son died after he claimed he'd rule over his brothers? Jacob wasn't going to chance losing a second son.

Benjamin's ten brothers had earned themselves a reputation for being untrustworthy—and years after the incident, Jacob remembered it.

Getting a reputation isn't hard. People quickly judge your worth based on things you've done and what they've heard about you. Sometimes a reputation isn't deserved. But most often we've earned most of what we've gotten.

When people look at you, do they see something Jesus would be proud of? As a Christian, your reputation isn't just your own—it belongs to Jesus too. People judge Him by your life.

I want others to see You in me, Lord, and I don't want to smudge the picture. Make me a trustworthy picture of Your love.

June 21

I will praise you, O LORD, among the nations; I will sing of you among the peoples. For great is your love, higher than the heavens; your faithfulness reaches to the skies.
PSALM 108:3–4

Some days, the praise just floats from your lips to God's ear. Whether it's your job, social life, or spiritual life, not a cloud troubles your skies. Maybe you've recently had a victory in one aspect of life, and you can't thank God enough.

Or maybe you're up to your ears in troubles, and you're stretched thin spiritually. Every day's become a challenge. *Praise* seems like a word meant for someone else.

Whether you've just seen God's salvation or you're holding on, depending on it, it's time to praise Him and tell the world of His faithfulness.

Your circumstances may have changed, but God hasn't. His love never left you, and He hasn't forgotten to be faithful. If times are good, you still need Him, and if times are rotten, you *know* you need Him even more.

Because you trust Him, tell of His faithfulness. Even if you can't see it yet, it's coming!

How can I thank You for Your faithfulness, Lord Jesus? Even when I don't see it, I know You're working for my good.

June 22

Our holy and glorious temple,
where our fathers praised you,
has been burned with fire,
and all that we treasured lies in ruins.
ISAIAH 64:11

The Jews didn't have a place to worship. Their bright temple lay in ruins. Gone were the golden implements that made worship a pleasure. All they valued lay in ruins.

Come on! Were these guys crazy? What meant so much to them? Stones? Golden bowls and candlesticks? Fine woven hangings?

Or God?

Though their building was ruined, their relationship with God didn't have to be. They couldn't offer blood sacrifices, but God hadn't reneged on the promise of a Messiah who would save them. If only they had trusted Him! If they drew close to God, *He* could become a heart treasure that nothing could destroy or carry away.

If you've lost your church building or had to leave a congregation you love, don't let despair overwhelm you. God and His promises stand firm.

Make Him your treasure, and no one can turn your spiritual life to rubble.

Lord, be the treasure of my life. You're more than buildings or even a group of Christians. I'm part of Your eternal church, made up of those who love You.

June 23

Love is patient, love is kind.
It does not envy, it does not boast,
it is not proud.
1 CORINTHIANS 13:4

If you're involved in a special romance, do you treat your beloved as someone who's exciting to be around? Probably. But do you also show your honey God's love by living out this verse?

Dating relationships can make emotions run high, but if you're constantly impatient with a date who's *never* on time or are unkind to one who's having a tough time seeing eye-to-eye with a family member, you're not reflecting God's love.

God doesn't rewrite the Book so we can act any way we want in our romances. Nowhere does God say we have a right to treat the ones closest to our hearts with less respect than a chance acquaintance or a close friend. When we really love, we treat each other with extraspecial gentleness and care.

If you can't treat a date with patience, kindness, and trust, reevaluate things. Your spiritual walk may be slipping. Or perhaps this isn't a person you're suited to, and you'd be better off as "just friends."

Lord, help me show Your love to anyone I date. Don't let me make my romantic life an exception to Your rules.

June 24

And Joseph's master took him, and put him into the prison, a place where the king's prisoners were bound: and he was there in the prison. But the LORD was with Joseph, and shewed him mercy, and gave him favour in the sight of the keeper of the prison.
GENESIS 39:20–21,KJV

Joseph didn't look for trouble—it just seemed to find him. First, his brothers sold him for a slave. Then his master's wife lied about him and got him tossed into prison.

If Joseph was favored by God so much, why wasn't his life smooth? we're tempted to ask. He didn't deserve what he got, especially not from Potiphar's wife.

The hard fact is that the wicked of this world don't live in a vacuum—they people the earth along with Christians, and sometimes Christians get hurt by their wrongdoing. When that happens, we cry out, "Life isn't fair!" And we're right—it isn't. But it wasn't fair, either, that Jesus had to come to earth for unbelievers and die to save them.

Are you ready to be treated unfairly for Him?

Lord, life isn't fair sometimes, but I still love You and want to serve You—even if it means getting mistreated by someone who doesn't know You.

June 25

A triple-braided cord is not easily broken.
ECCLESIASTES 4:12, NLT

A recent poll found that Christians with strong marriages attribute them to a strong prayer life.

What does prayer have to do with two jobs, a house, and two kids?

Couples who pray together regularly find that God becomes an interwoven third in their relationship. In the midst of seeking Him, a husband may uncover something that's been troubling him, but he couldn't seem to express. A wife may suddenly understand the reason for the tenseness that's filled her days. When they bring each trouble before God, solutions start.

Pour out your concerns together in prayer, and you'll learn a lot about your spouse, as well as God. The three cords—husband, wife, and Lord—become even more entwined, and two really do become one.

Tie the knot with Him.

Lord, I want my marriage to be tight with You and my spouse. Whomever I marry, let it be someone who spends time with You.

June 26

When times are good, be happy;
but when times are bad, consider:
God has made the one as well as the other.
Therefore, a man cannot discover
anything about his future.
ECCLESIASTES 7:14

Y ou can't predict the future. You can only plan to the best of your ability and move forward in faith.

So decide what kind of career you want. Work hard at it. But stay open to new ideas and truths along your path to success. Likewise, stay open to finding the mate God has for you, but don't put on a pith helmet and go hunting for one, or you'll turn romance away.

Despite all your good strategies, you'll run into a few roadblocks. Maybe your first career won't be as enjoyable as you'd expected, and you'll go back to school. Or you might wait a few extra years to meet Mr. or Ms. Right. But delays or detours don't have to end your trip.

Even your worst times aren't out of God's control. His master plan can't be circumvented. So enjoy the good days and know that the really bad ones can still lead you closer to God.

Take each day as it comes—a gift from Him.

Whether today is great or out of control, I trust in You, Lord.

June 27

And no wonder, for Satan himself
masquerades as an angel of light.
It is not surprising, then, if his servants
masquerade as servants of righteousness.
2 CORINTHIANS 11:14–15

In certain circles, you'll hear a lot of false ideas about angels. People often use them as a more comfortable replacement for God—one that will supposedly tell them about the future, but won't demand anything from them.

When you hear ideas about angels that don't agree with Scripture, look out! Remember, not only are there heavenly beings, hellish beings seek to deceive us daily.

How can you tell the difference? Look at the message the messenger bears. God's angels constantly serve Him. They don't try to take His place or detract attention from Him. They bring glory to God, not themselves.

When Satan's messengers face us, they can look good. Who wouldn't want a personal heavenly being at his or her command? But pride isn't a key to heaven, and any being that encourages it doesn't come from there, either.

Lord, thank You for Your angels who watch over us. But Satan's messengers I could do without. Keep me from the pride that hides truth from my eyes.

June 28

Finally, brethren, whatsoever things are true, whatsoever things are honest, whatsoever things are just, whatsoever things are pure, whatsoever things are lovely, whatsoever things are of good report; if there be any virtue, and if there be any praise, think on these things.
PHILIPPIANS 4:8, KJV

If you don't have a job yet, this *isn't* the time to spend your days in front of soap operas. They'll only make you depressed.

It's hard not to know where life's leading you, and negatives can easily permeate your thoughts. Doubts assail your mind when you don't have a clear-cut future. But when job-hunter's depression hangs over you, spend some *serious* time in prayer. You may not hear a voice from heaven say, "Here's the job, in this company, at this pay," but assurance that God is working for you will fill your heart. Hang on to that assurance when Satan tosses questions in your mind!

Don't give in to negative thinking. Instead, search out positives and focus on them. Spend a few hours in the evening doing things you enjoy and that lift your spirits.

But most of all, trust the God who made you to guide you in the right path.

When I don't know where I'm going, Lord, I can still hang on to You. Show me the way.

June 29

*I was forty years old when Moses
the servant of the Lord sent me from
Kadesh Barnea to explore the land.
And I brought him back a report
according to my convictions,
but my brothers who went up with me
made the hearts of the people melt with fear.*
JOSHUA 14:7–8

For forty-five years, Caleb waited for his real estate.

Years before, Moses had sent him to spy out the Promised Land. Caleb had faithfully called the Hebrews to enter the land. But terrorized by the negative reports of other spies, the people had refused. For forty-five years Caleb's reward was deferred, not through his own sin, but by that of others.

This hero of the faith could have ranted and raved and complained to God, "How come I have to suffer for *their* wrongdoing?" But as far as we know, Caleb didn't berate his fellow spies. Joshua 14 shows us a sweet-spirited, not bitter, man.

Caleb had a hero's attitude. He didn't look back to the past or point out others' obvious wrongs. He just kept following God.

Are you doing that today?

Lord, I've never had to wait forty-five years for anything. Keep me faithful, no matter how long You delay.

June 30

Honour thy father and thy mother,
as the LORD thy God hath commanded thee.
DEUTERONOMY 5:16, KJV

Since I moved out, my mom constantly calls me. Then the other day she dropped in and cleaned my apartment because she didn't think I'd done a good job. She thought she was doing me a favor, but I'm furious," Carla admitted.

You're stepping out, gaining independence, but Mom and Dad don't want to let go. Though you don't want to treat your parents disrespectfully, you *are* on your own. Ten years from now, you don't want Mom stopping by to clean!

Carla's mom didn't care so much how clean Carla's place was. She *really* wanted to spend time with her daughter, but when conversation lagged, Mom felt uncomfortable and started dusting. Once Carla discovered that, an occasional phone call let Mom know she was still loved. They met for lunch once in a while, and the relationship blossomed.

You can honor your parents without doing everything the way they do. Just treat them with respect and keep on loving them.

Lord, when my parents and I disagree, keep us communicating. I want to honor You and them.

July 1

For it is commendable if a man bears up
under the pain of unjust suffering
because he is conscious of God.
1 PETER 2:19

L ife is not totally just, and sometimes we find ourselves being punished for doing what we believe to be good. God considers bearing up in this situation commendable.

What does "bearing up" mean these days? In some instances it means continuing to live a faithful life at all costs, including martyrdom. In other cases, it just means paying the ticket we didn't deserve without a big fuss. Quite often it's easier to bear up under conditions that are severely unjust. It's obvious that you're being railroaded, and you receive the sympathy and admiration of others when you behave courageously. The little daily injustices of life are trickier and often harder to bear, but even then, it is commendable to persevere in doing what you know is right.

Father, help me bear up under unjust punishment in
every form and continue to live my life faithfully.

July 2

Whose adorning let it not be that outward adorning of plaiting the hair, and of wearing of gold, or of putting on of apparel; But let it be the hidden man of the heart, in that which is not corruptible, even the ornament of a meek and quiet spirit, which is in the sight of God of great price.
1 PETER 3:3–4, KJV

$\mathcal{S}$ome people would look great dressed in anything, with no makeup. The rest of us need a little help—and there's nothing wrong with looking your best. A few hours a week in the gym will not only tighten up your waistline but also leave you healthier and happier. A new dress or suit may make you more confident.

On the other hand, we all know perfectly gorgeous people whose souls live in a swamp. You may admire their appearance but wouldn't trust them to walk your dog. Their beauty is skin-deep—or less.

In the long run, it's performance that counts, which is exactly what this verse is saying. Do the best that you can with your outer self, but concentrate on the "unfading beauty of a gentle and quiet spirit" (NIV).

Lord, I will never be one of the beautiful people the world seems to favor, but I can develop the kind of inner beauty that You prefer. Thank You for judging me on the basis of how I live, not how I look.

July 3

What has been will be again,
what has been done will be done again;
there is nothing new under the sun.
ECCLESIASTES 1:9

We humans tend to be very territorial about our own time frame, impressed by any statement that begins, "Never before in history. . ." (add your own amazing fact). In matters of science, medicine, and space travel, these statements are often true and impressive. They make us feel special, better than our poor, uneducated ancestors who had to struggle along without moon rocks.

But in matters of human behavior, good or bad, there really is nothing new under the sun. We have a finite number of human responses to any situation we may encounter, and they don't vary too much from the responses available throughout human history. If it's human, it's been done before. The only thing new is the magnitude of our actions today. We can do things faster now, on a grander scale, and instant communication makes our every action seem new and novel.

Father, the next time I feel as though my suffering is unique, remind me of my long line of ancestors who dealt with the same problem and somehow survived it. You were there for them and will be there for me, too.

July 4

Blessed is the nation whose God is the LORD.
PSALM 33:12

We don't have a state religion because our forefathers who lived under a state religion experienced it as oppressive, limiting individual freedom. While it might be efficient to have one religion for all, we just won't line up like sheep going through a gate. It's not in our character. We're a nation of fence jumpers.

Were our forefathers great examples of godliness? Probably not. They broke the same commandments we do, just as often as we do. The fact that the press didn't follow them around with a telephoto lens probably helped their reputation, though.

It would be inaccurate to say that our country follows the Lord God today and is blessed because of it. As a political unit, it doesn't, but as individuals, we can. Those who prize religious freedom are still free to be as good as they can be, to apply religious principles to their own lives anytime they want to, and to build a nation where the Lord God is free to reign in *their* hearts.

Father, thank You for the many freedoms we enjoy in this country. Help us build a righteous nation, one person at a time.

July 5

Seek the peace and prosperity of the city
to which I have carried you into exile.
Pray to the LORD for it,
because if it prospers, you too will prosper.
JEREMIAH 29:7

Our hearts always know where our home is, especially if we're not living there. Although we may yearn to be elsewhere, we have to make do with where we are. We never have to give up the dream of returning home someday, but we do have to live in the present, and it is wise to invest in our current home. Making this town a better place to live is to our own advantage, both psychologically and financially.

Have you registered to vote in your current location? Have you found a church to attend, a doctor, and a dentist? Do you shop locally or put off buying what you need until you return to your "real" home? Do you do volunteer work? Have you made some local friends? It may be decades before you can live in the place your heart calls home. Don't waste years dreaming of somewhere else when you can contribute where you are now.

Father, show me how I can help out wherever I'm living right now.

July 6

"For I know the plans I have for you,"
says the LORD, "They are plans for good and not
for disaster, to give you a future and a hope."
JEREMIAH 29:11, NLT

We all have plans for our future, even if they're a little vague. We know whether we want to marry and have children, places we want to go, and things we hope to accomplish. Most of us are realistic about our plans, knowing some will work out and some won't. We also know our plans will change from year to year as we mature and see more of the world.

What we don't like is to have our plans blown out of the water and to have our lives take a sudden change of direction. There's nothing more frightening than losing the anchor that's been holding our life in place and being forced to start over again.

Fortunately, some of these disasters turn out to be blessings. Even when we have no idea which way to turn, the Lord knows where we're going and will keep us on the right path, even if the trip's a little bumpy.

Father, when my life suddenly turns upside down,
I will trust in You to lead me in the right direction.

July 7

*Seldom set foot in your
neighbor's house—too much of you,
and he will hate you.*
PROVERBS 25:17

This verse isn't saying you should avoid your neighbors or refrain from having a social life with them. The Bible is full of verses that applaud neighborliness and caring for others. But there are limits. Some neighborhoods are remarkably close and friendly; others aren't. When you move into a new neighborhood, you need to learn the neighborhood rules and not be a pest when people want to be left alone.

A similar problem involves a group of friends who begin to marry. When the old gang begins to break up, it's easy to blame the new spouses instead of admitting that you are part of the problem. If you want to stay close, you'd be wise to become friends with the new spouses and give the couple the space they need, so neither will hate you.

Father, give me the good sense to allow my friends the space they need and to realize that relationships change with time.

July 8

Listen, for I have worthy things to say;
I open my lips to speak what is right.
PROVERBS 8:6

You can't always keep your mouth shut. Sometimes others really need your help. You may already have gone through a problem they're facing now and have some good advice on how to get through it.

On a larger scale, you may want your opinion heard on a local, national, or international issue. You may feel compelled to join a group working for a cause you believe in. Don't be afraid to wade in and speak your piece. You may be young, but you're not stupid. If you feel you have something to contribute, have faith in yourself and do it. You have to pay your dues, actually and figuratively, but once people see you pulling your weight, they will begin to listen when you have a good idea you just can't keep to yourself.

Lord, I do have things I want to say. Give me the courage to say them, and help me earn the respect of others, so my voice will be heard.

July 9

*He who works his land
will have abundant food,
but the one who chases fantasies
will have his fill of poverty.*
PROVERBS 28:19

Two or three generations ago, young people were advised, "Learn a trade and you'll always have work." This was during the Depression, and the advice was good, just as the verse above is good advice. Society changes, and the available jobs change with it. Today it's a good idea to know your way around the Internet and a computer keyboard. Who knows what new jobs will open up in the next twenty years?

All vocational advice is based on the same premise: Pick a job, do it well, and don't chase fantasies. This doesn't mean you shouldn't dream of a better job, but it should be a realistic dream, attainable through education or experience.

Go ahead and dream, but back your dream up with productive work, just in case.

Lord, I have so many dreams and hopes. Some will come true and some won't. Teach me the difference between dreams and fantasies and lead me into the work You have designed for me.

July 10

For I am God, and not man;
the Holy One in the midst of thee.
HOSEA 11:9, KJV

We have to be careful not to confuse human beings with God. Humanity was made in God's image, but we're only a tiny little reflection of all He
is. We see our limits every day and tend to apply
them to God. It's a perfectly human thing to do,
although inaccurate.

We tend to give God human characteristics.
When nature devastates part of the world, we think
God must be angry at someone. When a great discovery brings a company wealth, we say God is
pleased with the company. Bad things happen to
good people; good things happen to the evil. How
can we say God is wrong in either case?

The Holy One among us is God, not human.
Sometimes He is a mystery to us, and we might as
well admit that and stop trying to make Him more
like ourselves.

Father, I cannot begin to imagine Your glory and
power. Be patient when I limit You in my mind.

July 11

*Even a fool is thought wise if he keeps silent,
and discerning if he holds his tongue.*
PROVERBS 17:28

There's far too much information out there these days. Whatever happened to discernment and discretion? What happened to the vital concept of innocent until proven guilty? Why do entertainers and the press assume we care about private matters made public? Don't these people have more important matters to discuss?

Don't think that this overemphasis on private matters doesn't affect the average person's life, either. How many dedicated, intelligent people will run for public office on even the local level once they realize that the foolish acts of their youth will be fodder for the campaign? Do you really need to know the candidates' intimate personal mistakes?

The truth is, a lot of stuff we simply do not need to know about. Conservatives and liberals alike have a personal comfort level that's being assaulted today. Not only does this assault make us uneasy, it's also diverting attention from the huge amount of work that needs doing in the world.

Mom was right: "Mind your own business" and "Hold your tongue."

Father, the public's need to know is being perverted today. Keep my mind centered on the issues that really count, not in the gutter.

July 12

You, then, why do you judge your brother?
Or why do you look down on your brother?
For we will all stand before
God's judgment seat.
ROMANS 14:10

Are you absolutely sure you know the mind of God? Can you judge others on the basis of what you know today? More important, whom do *you* want to be judged by? Look at our court system, where the guilty often go free and the innocent suffer. Would you trust that system with your ultimate judgment?

Yet we go on judging others every day of our lives. We do have to make some important choices. Some people we don't want to associate with for one reason or another, so to a certain extent, we do have to judge. Where we get into trouble is when we condemn. It's one thing to avoid someone whose actions we disapprove of, but condemning him or her is something else. We aren't equipped for that job, since no one knows the full story of another's life. "Do not condemn, and you will not be condemned" (Luke 6:37).

Father, help me in the daily choices I must make, but remind me that judgment is Yours to administer, not mine.

July 13

*They think it strange that you do not plunge
with them into the same flood of dissipation,
and they heap abuse on you.*
1 PETER 4:4

Some graduates go a little crazy once they're free of parental limits. If Dad's not around to smell their breath at the front door, they think drinking to excess is perfectly acceptable. Mom's not standing at the foot of the stairs, so it must be okay to take a date to their room. The moral police aren't in residence anymore.

It's true—they aren't. No one is going to impose moral behavior on you, short of criminal acts. You're on your own. It's a learning experience we all have to go through, and some can't handle the sudden freedom and responsibility.

Unfortunately, a lot of these moral toddlers are popular and powerful; they *will* heap abuse on you if you try to live a moral life. It will confuse you and may cause you to stumble, but you need to be strong. Eventually, these children will grow up and realize you were right and they were wrong. Until then, hang in there.

Father, give me the strength to follow my own values, not those of others.

July 14

*Avoid godless, foolish discussions with those
who oppose you with their
so-called knowledge.*
1 TIMOTHY 6:20, NLT

Young adulthood is the time to decide what you do and do not believe to be true. It's a time to question everything, reject some old things, and embrace some new things. It's a time that makes parents worry, because they know you will be looking critically at their beliefs, too.

You have to do this. You can't blindly accept everything you hear. You have to make your own decisions and be prepared to live with them or you'll be a wishy-washy nobody.

You also have to learn discernment. That's what Paul was warning Timothy about. Some positions must be taken on faith. All the talk in the world can't prove the unprovable, so look at everything carefully before you decide to embrace a stand, but realize that some things just have to be accepted on faith, not facts.

Father, no one seems to agree on anything, including faith. Give me discernment and the courage to stand by my beliefs, even if I can't prove they are correct.

July 15

*"I am sending you out like sheep among wolves.
Therefore be as shrewd as snakes
and as innocent as doves."*
MATTHEW 10:16

The disciples were being sent out to spread the word of Jesus and do His work, but first Jesus gave them extensive instructions. A lot of people didn't want to hear their message. They would be rejected, reviled, and in physical danger. It was very much like sending a flock of sheep out to graze the hills where wolves prowl, and Jesus must have wondered how many of them He would see again.

But He didn't tell them to be fools. They were to be as pure and innocent as doves, but also as shrewd as a snake. This wasn't a kamikaze mission, by any means. They were to watch their backs and use cunning to survive their mission, because Jesus had future plans for them.

We tend to forget this part of Jesus' instructions, perhaps because we think it's impossible to be innocent and careful at the same time.

Father, You alone know what will be asked of me in the future, but I trust in You and know You will give me my instructions when the time comes for me to do Your work.

July 16

When tempted, no one should say,
"God is tempting me."
For God cannot be tempted by evil,
nor does he tempt anyone.
JAMES 1:13

In other words, Flip Wilson was right when he said, "The devil made me do it," although he was just using the devil to excuse his own actions.

We're all tempted now and then, and when we are, we try to blame someone else. Sometimes we blame another human, our own human weaknesses, the devil, or even God. But God *never* tempts anyone. At the most, He might allow us to be tempted by someone else, but other than taking this hands-off approach, He is blameless.

It's not that God is unable to tempt us. There's no doubt He could do a bang-up job of it, if He wanted to, but He doesn't. So when you goof up, don't place the blame in the wrong place. Most of the time, you did yourself in.

God will not tempt you, but He will help when others do, so before you go ahead and make the wrong choice, ask for His help, which He gives freely and with love.

Father, thank You for Your care and love, which will enable me to resist the temptations that come my way.

July 17

*A perverse man stirs up dissension,
and a gossip separates close friends.*
PROVERBS 16:28

Finding and keeping good friends is hard work. You go through a lot of acquaintances before you find one friend you can trust totally and be honest with. Then, once you find him or her, you have to work at staying friends.

One of the best ways to lose a friend is to listen to gossip: "You know what he said about you?" The only proper answer to this question is, "No, and I don't want to hear about it from you." You never know the intentions of a gossip, and it's foolish to listen to one. If you have a problem with a friend, it should stay between the two of you until you work it out. No third party is going to help. Refuse to listen to gossip about a friend if you value the friendship.

Lord, gossip can sometimes be fun, but more often it's dangerous. Give me the good sense to ignore it and deal honestly with my friends in all things.

July 18

Owe no man any thing.
ROMANS 13:8, KJV

How many credit cards did you receive in the mail before you graduated? Banks routinely send shiny new cards out to seniors, all "preapproved." Just sign the form and you're an adult, often before you have a job. Sure, the credit limit is pretty low, but in a year or so it will be mysteriously raised to a level you can't possibly afford.

Your first credit card is a rite of passage. Someone actually trusts you to pay your bills! And it's certainly handy. So accept one of the many offered if you feel you need it, but don't fall into the trap of accepting five or six of them, or you'll never be able to pay them all off when the bills come in.

If you can't pay a credit card bill in full when it's due, you shouldn't be using a card at all. A fistful of fully loaded cards, paid off with minimum monthly payments, will never have a zero balance. You don't need that. You could take the interest you will have to pay, invest it in a mutual fund, and double your money before your credit card will be paid off. It's better to do without than to fall into the credit trap.

Father, teach me how to handle my money wisely and not spend more than I earn at this stage of my life.

July 19

Give everyone what you owe him:
If you owe taxes, pay taxes;
if revenue, then revenue;
if respect, then respect;
if honor, then honor.
ROMANS 13:7

There are lots of kinds of debt, and only some of them involve cash. Remember the one teacher you connected with who influenced your whole life? You wouldn't think of sending her a check to repay your debt to her. You owe her honor, not cash. How about the policeman who spent his valuable time talking to you when you got into a little trouble and showed you a better way to go? He deserves your respect, not a tip.

Money debts are pretty easy to deal with. You pay them off once and they're history. It's the debts of honor and respect that last a lifetime and require real work to pay off. Some of them mean so much to you that they will never be paid in full. So the next time you pay off your credit card, take a few moments to remember your other debts and thank God that those people were there when you needed them.

Lord, remind me of those I owe respect and honor to, and show me the best way to repay those debts.

July 20

I do not understand what I do.
For what I want to do I do not do,
but what I hate I do.
ROMANS 7:15

Paul was as human as the rest of us and not afraid to admit it. "I don't know why I act the way I do," he said. "I don't do the things I want to do. Instead, I do what I don't want to do."

We don't know what Paul's sins were, but they really bugged him, and it seems he never conquered them, although he obviously worked on them a lot. His standards for himself were probably pretty high.

You set yourself up to fail if you think you should be perfect. Are you better than Paul was? Have a little mercy on yourself.

This doesn't mean you should use Paul's failure as an excuse to run wild or not even try to control yourself. Paul conquered a good portion of his weaknesses, and you can do the same. Pick out one of your least-favorite behaviors and concentrate on it for a while. You may be surprised—but don't expect perfection.

Lord, my sins are numerous and my strengths are few. Help me be the best I can be and trust Your forgiveness for the rest.

July 21

The Bible is talking about worship here, suggesting that a certain amount of order should be maintained during services, but it's easy enough to see how the same idea can have wider application. After all, if a worship service can be turned into disorder, imagine what we can do the rest of the week.

Some of us are more comfortable with disorder than others. A few thrive on it, feeling it keeps them on their toes. Others can't stand disorder and feel frustrated or insecure when faced with it.

Let's face it, we're a pretty disorderly bunch. We don't have the discipline of ants or bees, and who would want it? We tend to throw our dirty socks on the floor and neglect to take out the garbage. We like a little disorder now and then.

But when it comes to work, we need order and routine. Reports need to be written on time, tools need to be cleaned and put away, work has to be prioritized or nothing will get done. Leave your fondness for disorder at home and be as organized as possible at work.

Father, I'm not the most orderly person in my private life, but teach me how to be organized at work.

July 22

Unto Adam also and to his wife did the LORD God make coats of skins, and clothed them.
GENESIS 3:21, KJV

This verse comes right after God cursed Adam and Eve and right before He chased them out of Eden. Smack dab in the middle of all the thundering and armed angels, God took some animal skins and did a little sewing. What's going on here?

Well, that's parenting for you. How many times did your mom yell at you, then turn around and bake cookies before she finished her lecture? How many times did your father tell you to be more careful with your money and then hand you a twenty before he told you what *not* to spend it on?

The next time you're ready to blow up at someone, follow God's example. Take a break. Do a little something to show you care for the person, and let your love defuse your anger.

Father, thank You for Your unfailing love when I goof up. Your anger would be more than I could stand.

July 23

See how the farmer waits for the land
to yield its valuable crop
and how patient he is for
the autumn and spring rains.
JAMES 5:7

If there's one thing a farmer knows well, it's patience. You can't hurry a plant's growth, and you can't do a thing to bring the rain. Standing in the field and looking at the sky is often all that can be done.

It's hard to be patient in an instant world. You need to shake off that cold right now, but your nose is still going to run for five days unless you take so much medicine you can't function. A baby comes when it comes, conveniently or not. The puppy will be housebroken when it decides to be, so don't buy a new rug yet. Nature has a way of telling us we're not the hotshots we think we are.

We have to remember that although we can control a lot of our life, there's a lot more we can't do anything about, and there's no sense in getting upset about what we can't control. The rains will come.

Father, teach me patience when I'm faced with something I cannot control. There is enough that I can work on to keep me busy until the time is right.

July 24

*Perseverance must finish its work
so that you may be mature and complete,
not lacking anything.*
JAMES 1:4

We don't often think of perseverance as a blessing or something beneficial to our growth. We persevere because the only other options are defeat or retreat. We do not go out looking for the chance to persevere; it usually involves unpleasant experiences.

Whether or not we want these experiences, they will come. The requirements of our job may be beyond our capabilities, yet we persevere and eventually learn how to handle the work. Losing the twenty pounds we put on at college seems to go on forever, yet we lose a little every week and eventually get there.

Perseverance is tiny little steps toward a goal, not one valiant effort that solves the problem immediately. It teaches patience, planning, and working for future rewards instead of instant gratification—all things that lead to maturity and completeness.

Father, perseverance is hard work, no matter what the goal is. Give me the patience and foresight I need to persevere and mature.

July 25

*My conscience is clear,
but that does not make me innocent.*
1 CORINTHIANS 4:4

Paul knew the difference between his conscience and the truth. As far as he knew, he was in the clear —no guilt, no worry. Most of us would be delighted just to be able to honestly claim the first half of this verse.

Then he went and added the second half, "but that does not make me innocent." Paul understood that our conscience has little to do with real guilt or innocence. Our conscience is the way we see ourselves and may have nothing in common with the way God sees us. Only God understands our motivation. It's possible to live a good life for all the wrong reasons. Are we good because we love God or because we fear Him? Do we serve others out of love or ambition? Do we sing as praise or performance?

Paul knew it is foolish for us to even try to judge ourselves. The final judgment is God's.

Father, You are the only Judge I need to answer to. Only You know the real me, and I count on Your guidance every day.

July 26

*Accept Christians who are weak in faith,
and don't argue with them about what
they think is right or wrong.*
ROMANS 14:1, NLT

People have differing levels of faith. Some talk about their faith, others keep their beliefs to themselves. Some follow every rule they can find, while others skip around and choose the rules they think are vital. Faith is as individual as those who profess it.

Some matters are indisputable, but others provide a little leeway for interpretation. Did early Christian converts from Judaism have to obey the laws of Moses? Did Gentiles have to be circumcised? Was any food unclean? These questions caused a lot of controversy within the church, and it took years to answer them.

Meanwhile, the church continued to grow because converts were accepted as they were. Belief in Jesus was necessary; other matters were secondary. Since then, we've become divided over many other questions, some of which may never be settled. In the meantime, "accept him whose faith is weak."

Father, teach me what is vital and what is not, and help me accept lovingly those with differing opinions.

July 27

Rejoice with those who rejoice;
mourn with those who mourn.
ROMANS 12:15

Have you noticed how short our attention span has become? Our movies have to have constant action. The same thing goes for books: Don't bother to show us the setting unless someone's lurking in the shadows. Life's too short for character development.

We do the same thing in our personal relationships. Listening is a lost art. Now when we're silent it's because we're waiting our turn to speak, not listening to what the other person is saying. As a result, the only person we truly relate to is ourselves.

That's not what friendship is supposed to be like. It takes time and patience to be a friend. You have to really listen, because often real feelings come out slowly, a bit at a time. How can you rejoice with someone when you have no idea what makes him happy? How can you mourn with a friend when you never knew her mother was dying?

Try being a good listener for a few months and watch your circle of friends expand. You'll never be alone in a crowd again.

Father, teach me to be a good listener, someone with the patience to hear a story to its end and really try to understand.

July 28

I said, "Oh, that I had the wings of a dove!
I would fly away and be at rest."
PSALM 55:6

When we start sounding like the writer of this psalm, it's time for a vacation. How wonderful it would be to just fly away and rest whenever our hearts and minds were sick of it all—but we have to have our vacation time approved at work, find the "perfect" place to go, put down a deposit, arrange transportation, and buy the clothes we'll need. Sometimes it doesn't seem worth the bother or expense.

Some companies insist their employees take their vacation time, for good reasons. Vacations are about the only time we can completely relax and do whatever we want to do. Just looking forward to a planned vacation gives us a little mental rest—a "mental adjustment" that motivates us in our work.

The job will not fall apart while we're away. All in all, flying away now and then makes us better at our work the rest of the year. Enjoy.

Father, help me let go of my work and learn to enjoy the vacations I deserve, whether I spend them at home or thousands of miles away.

July 29

*In repentance and rest is your salvation,
in quietness and trust is your strength,
but you would have none of it.*
ISAIAH 30:15

Sometimes we are our own worst enemies. We run away from so many things that frighten us, trusting our fears more than the Lord who protects and shelters us.

Some fear commitment so much that they drive away those they love. Others are so worried about money that they never enjoy anything without first checking the price tag. Fear of losing a job keeps some from showing any initiative or creativity, which in itself can endanger their jobs.

The world is full of fearsome things, and a certain amount of caution is required, but there's no reason to let fear run our lives. Maturity and achievement come to those who know how to take a few chances. Sometimes you get bitten by a strange dog; most of the time, he licks your hand.

Trust the Lord with your life and step out in courage and strength.

Father, thank You for Your love and care every day of my life. Help me trust You for my safety, which will let me live in quietness and strength.

July 30

*You should not look
down on your brother in the day
of his misfortune.*
OBADIAH 12

It's hard not to gloat when things turn out better for ourselves than for others, especially when we've always been the underdog. Class reunions bring out these feelings in us. The star football player turned to fat, and the cheerleaders have all had to resort to hair coloring, and we feel somehow justified by both events. These small examples of justice make us feel good.

But fortune is pretty fickle, and if we gloat, we'd better do it discretely, because life is long, and the worm does turn. Everything will be different at the next reunion. Besides, the guy who looks like a failure now may be totally happy, while those who succeeded are miserable. You just never know. Looking down on others for any reason is futile, not to mention unchristian.

Father, only You know who is successful in life, and Your standards are not the same as mine. Teach me not to judge others on the basis of worldly fortune.

July 31

I will pay that that I have vowed.
JONAH 2:9, KJV

Jonah proved that welshing on a promise made to God is a bad idea. He tried to run away from such a promise and almost died before he changed his mind (admittedly under pressure) and renewed his vow. Fortunately, this time he kept his word.

Yet we go on making promises to God today and breaking them tomorrow. We also break the promises we make to others. In neither case are we tossed off boats and saved by sea creatures, but you have to believe that God's not exactly pleased by our failures.

Promises should never be taken lightly. You can break a person's heart by breaking a promise. You can lose a job, be drummed out of military service, or never be trusted again. Never promise more than you can deliver.

Father, make me think before I promise anything to anyone. If I can't keep a promise, I should never make it in the first place.

August 1

In the heavens he has pitched a tent for the sun. . . .
It rises at one end of the heavens and
makes its circuit to the other;
nothing is hidden from its heat.
PSALM 19:4, 6

If you haven't thought of the sun the rest of the year, in the summer you become very aware of it.

The Old Testament peoples couldn't avoid its harsh rays, either. The sun stared them in the face day after day. It was an important part of their lives, nurturing crops or drying them to a crisp.

Many ancient peoples created sun gods. When they couldn't explain why the crops shriveled up, they'd blame their supposed "god."

The Israelites didn't have a collection of deities for every part of the universe. They knew God created the sun, and what they took on faith put them ahead of their time. Science agreed: Today anyone worshipping a sun god looks silly.

People don't tend to think of Christians as being ahead of their time. You're more likely to be called old-fashioned, naive, or bigoted. Like the ancient Israelites, are you ready to look ridiculous to the world if it means being faithful to God?

Maybe, in the end, you'll be ahead of your time.

Lord God, I don't care what the world thinks as long as I'm faithful to You. I don't want to be behind the times in Your eyes.

August 2

*Keep your servant also from willful sins;
may they not rule over me.*
PSALM 19:13

Because you're a Christian, you want to serve Jesus. He saved you from so much, and you're grateful. Why, if you could give Him the whole world, it wouldn't be enough.

What if He asked you to give up your car, career, or girlfriend? Would you still be keen to serve? A lot of Christians wouldn't be.

We say we want to serve Jesus, but do we? Do we tell Him we'll witness, but we won't talk to our friends? Do we want to serve only behind the scenes and never give a testimony?

Only willful servants identify the gifts they feel comfortable with and try to make God use them. Real servants take the place He commands.

Witnessing to friends or giving a public testimony may seem impossible. *I could never do that,* you may think.

Alone, you probably never would. But you don't have to rely on yourself. You can rely on Him to enable you to do anything He calls you to do.

Today God may call you to serve in areas that seem nearly impossible. If so, take on that task. When it looks most impossible, His grace will be at hand.

Set your tasks before me, Your servant, Lord. I know Your enabling power will come.

August 3

Peter and the other apostles knew God's promises. Two Scriptures implied that Judas's place should be filled. So they shopped around, found two likely replacements, prayed that God would choose between *their* two choices, and filled the spot with Matthias.

Scripture never again mentions Matthias.

Those well-meaning apostles had rushed to fill the empty slot in their "church board" and chose the wrong man.

How could they have chosen the right one? Saul, Christian persecutor, hardly seemed to fit the bill.

It took time—and God's timing—to make Saul into an apostle. He had to come face-to-face with Jesus and experience conversion. The "new man," Paul, was the perfect person to bring the gospel to a tough bunch of Gentiles.

Like Peter and his friends, we often rush to do "God's work" in our way.

Have you prayed *and* waited for God's answer?

I want to obey You, Jesus. Show me Your plan, not my own.

August 4

*He did not leave a man or woman alive
to be brought to Gath, for he thought,
"They might inform on us and say,
'This is what David did.'"
And such was his practice as long as
he lived in Philistine territory.*
1 SAMUEL 27:11

David had become so popular that King Saul considered him a threat to his kingdom. What better usurper than Israel's popular military leader?

As death threatened, David took his warriors away. They hired themselves out as mercenaries to the Philistines—one of Israel's enemies. David didn't want to attack the Israelites or their allies. So he'd go out and attack Israel's enemies. At the end of the day, he'd lie to Achish, the Philistine king, about his work.

Caught in sin's web, David knew he had to kill everyone in each town he raided. If a single person reported on his real actions, it could have cost David his life.

David agonized about being caught out. Had he gotten everyone?

We know David's trapped feeling. He couldn't admit his wrongs, yet he couldn't stop.

Only God's forgiveness cuts sin's web.

Need some web-cutting today? Turn to the Master.

Lord, untangle me from sin's web. I don't want to be tied up anymore.

August 5

*I have been blameless before him
and have kept myself from sin.*
2 SAMUEL 22:24

Who can claim never to have sinned, to have been blameless before God? Certainly not David, unless he suddenly became very forgetful of his own life—adultery with Bathsheba and the murder of Uriah the Hittite, to mention only two high points.

Is David kidding himself? *Blameless* isn't the word we connect with him. In fact, many of us are comforted by the fact that God could still love a man who sinned more than we think we have.

David hadn't forgotten his own failings. If he'd had to depend on himself, he would have been lost.

Instead he knew that God was looking into his heart. David desired the ability to obey perfectly. He knew he didn't, but, oh, how he wished he could.

He looked to God to make up the gap between desire and reality. Graciously, God responded and, through the work of Messiah, made David completely perfect.

Do you seek perfection today? Turn to the Savior.

Lord, I know I can't be perfect under my own power. I need Your Son's holiness today.

August 6

"I am with you and will save you,"
declares the LORD. "Though I completely destroy
all the nations among which I scatter you,
I will not completely destroy you."
JEREMIAH 30:11

*B*abylon. Not a name you read in the *New York Times*. *Newsweek* doesn't mention it, either. Why? Because Babylon fell centuries ago.

But you'll read all about Israel.

God promised the Jews who were facing exile in Babylon that He'd never destroy them. Then the Lord split up His people, sending them as slaves into a foreign land. Years later, their conquering country, Babylon, fell, but conquered Israel returned to life.

Israel didn't always exist as a nation. For centuries, Jews were spread all over the world, with no homeland. But God hadn't deserted the people He'd called to Himself. He promised to bring her back, and in 1948, He did.

God remained faithful to a promise He made to a rebellious people He was punishing for their sin. Will He be less faithful to you?

Imagine the promises one *faithful* person could see Him fulfill!

Faithfulness like Yours, Lord, amazes me. Even when I fail You, You don't desert me. Keep me faithful to You today.

August 7

For ye have heard of my conversation
in past time in the Jews' religion,
how that beyond measure I persecuted
the church of God, and wasted it.
GALATIANS 1:13, KJV

Before becoming a Christian, Bette had been sexually involved with a number of guys, and people knew it.

Once she knew God, Bette struggled with that sin and began to gain victory over it.

But when her youth group wanted to start an outreach to her classmates, Bette balked at the idea of helping out. "You don't understand, I have a reputation there. It makes no difference that I'm a Christian. Plenty of people still point a finger at me."

Her pastor, knowing how much Bette had changed, still wanted her to give her testimony. "It will be a challenge," he admitted. "But I think you can take it on. You can't run away from the past, so tell people about it. You have a great testimony to share."

If you have an embarrassing past you've gained victory over, don't fear it. Paul had one, too. Instead of hiding his persecution of the church, he let God use it to bring Him glory.

Some may have pointed, but more believed.

Lord, You've worked a miracle in my life. Don't let me be shy in sharing what You've done.

August 8

I pray that you may be active in
sharing your faith, so that
you will have a full understanding of
every good thing we have in Christ.
PHILEMON 6

Gina met Jesus through a friend whose church was having trouble. Since her friend didn't want to bring a new Christian to church with her, Gina didn't know where to go. After trying a church or two, she just gave up.

Gina loved God and could feel a change in her heart, but it was just her and Jesus, alone against the world.

That's a sad Christian life.

God made believers to be part of a Christian community. Share your faith, but connect a new Christian with a strong church, too. Don't leave a baby Christian out in the cold.

Forest-ranger Christians, unconnected with churches, can't share a faith that's been deepened by a sense of community. None of us grows alone, so usually we *don't* grow.

Reach out to unbelievers, but also reach in to your brothers and sisters in Christ. Then you'll really have something to share.

I need a strong church, Lord. Draw me to share the best news in my life.

August 9

Woe! Woe, O great city,
where all who had ships on the sea
became rich through her wealth!
In one hour she has been brought to ruin!
REVELATION 18:19

Wealth! We don't often think of ourselves as having it. The other guy is usually the one who gets "the breaks," has a nicer home, or got on the "fast track" faster.

Revelation 18 seems to describe a whole city of "fast-trackers." Even those in the lowest 1 percent income bracket there could have great homes, hefty bank accounts, and drive the latest cars.

God warns us that not just personal possessions, but also beautiful office buildings, wonderful government services, and fancy department stores don't last. They're just as fragile as our smaller bank accounts, clunky cars, and condos. One hour, and poof, that city's gone.

Things don't last, but Jesus does. That's the message in the Bible's last book.

Love Him today, and you'll last, too.

Though I'd like nice things, I don't want them more than an eternity with You, Lord. No matter how much I own, make it all Yours.

August 10

*They are darkened in their understanding
and separated from the life of God
because of the ignorance that is in them
due to the hardening of their hearts.*
EPHESIANS 4:18

Ross didn't know how many times he and Kevin had talked about the world's beginning, the environment, and recent scientific discoveries. But their discussions always reached an impasse. No matter how clear his arguments were, Ross felt his friend just wouldn't accept them. Instead Kevin held fast to a few illogical beliefs, no matter how hard Ross tried to show him how wrong they were.

Showing a non-Christian how wrong he is can be a deadly witnessing tool. It rarely works, because, like Kevin, he'll become defensive. Then you don't have a chance to discover the real objections.

Kevin's problem wasn't really with the world. Years ago he had decided he didn't believe in God, who didn't seem to answer one childhood prayer. All Ross's logic didn't deal with that heartfelt issue.

Have a friend with a heart problem? Don't try to convince him. Instead pray for him and show him Jesus' love until his heart is opened.

Lord, soften the hearts of my non-Christian friends and family members. Work in Your Spirit where I can't touch.

August 11

*And Hushai said unto Absalom, "Nay;
but whom the LORD, and this people,
and all the men of Israel, choose, his will I be,
and with him will I abide. And again,
whom should I serve? should I not serve in the
presence of his son? as I have served in thy
father's presence, so will I be in thy presence."*
2 SAMUEL 16:18–19, KJV

Hushai got caught right in the middle of a political war between King David and his son Absalom. Because he needed information on his son's doings, David asked his friend to stay in Jerusalem after Absalom took over. So Hushai became David's inside man in Jerusalem.

Despite his dangerous position, Hushai spoke the truth to would-be-king Absalom. Up front he said he'd serve the one God had chosen. Was it Hushai's fault that David's proud son thought that was *him?* Hushai *did* serve Absalom by giving him the truth.

Hushai was in a position much like the corporate worker who tells his boss the truth he doesn't want to hear. It was right, but it wouldn't make him popular.

If the falsehoods of office politics threaten you, stand firm, like Hushai. You'll be serving One even greater than your boss.

Lord, I don't want office politics to blind me to Your will. Keep me in Your truth.

August 12

If we confess our sins,
he is faithful and just and
will forgive us our sins and
purify us from all unrighteousness.
1 JOHN 1:9

You might call this a Christian's independence verse.

Before you were a Christian, even when you really wanted to walk in the right way, you had a hard time of it. Wrongdoing dogged your footsteps, and when you managed to do good, it somehow got messed up.

Maybe you tried to help an acquaintance, but it turned out wrong. Later, you wished you hadn't because doing right meant you had to bear the consequences—like an unwanted "friend."

But turning from your sins, through confession, and receiving God's heart purification gave you new light on doing right. The price for right actions might still be high, but you know why you're paying it. You're serving Jesus, and God cleans it all up in the end.

Now you're free to do right and take the consequences—because Jesus has already paid for them.

Doing the right thing can be so difficult, Lord. Sometimes I wonder why, if it's right, things don't go right. Keep Your great plan before me.

August 13

And we know that in all things God works
for the good of those who love him,
who have been called
according to his purpose.
ROMANS 8:28

I guess we're just going to have to Romans 8:28 this," Jack's pastor commented when he faced troubles. Jack liked the expression and knew immediately what Pastor Steve meant. They were just going to have to trust that God knew what He was doing and that He remained in control. In the end, God would bring good out of the worst situation.

Are you in a situation that needs Romans 8:28-ing? Maybe you just lost your job because of company downsizing. Or your plans for more schooling fell through. Can you trust God for His timing? Maybe He has a better job that you never would have looked for otherwise. Perhaps there's a different type of schooling in your future. Wait for Him, and He'll show you the way.

When troubles come calling, trust the God who can work *anything* out for people whom He's called to serve Him. He has a plan for each believer's life.

Are you following that plan today?

Lord, I know Your plan is best for my future. Help me walk in it hour by hour.

August 14

God's love is so wonderful; have you ever wondered why everyone doesn't want it?

For some reason beyond our understanding, God doesn't need everyone to accept Him. He isn't in a divine popularity contest. He'd rather have a few good people to do His bidding than masses of disobedient servants.

He created plenty of Israelites. Centuries ago there were so many of them that Pharaoh made them slaves. They'd multiplied so well, they were outnumbering the Egyptians! And they haven't died out since.

But God didn't make a rubber-stamp salvation that said, "You're an Israelite, so into the kingdom you come!" He wanted people with committed hearts who would stand the test. Gentile or Jew, it wasn't the background, but the heart that mattered.

If you know Him, He chose you out of millions of people. He wants you to serve Him because you're special to Him. There's a place for you in His kingdom, if your heart is His.

How could you choose me, Lord, out of millions of people on this planet? I'm honored to be part of Your remnant. Show me how to serve You today.

August 15

I do well to be angry, even unto death.
JONAH 4:9, KJV

Sometimes God does something we really don't like. Perhaps a friend's mom dies or a cousin's girl jilts him. It doesn't seem right, and anger fills us. *How could You do this?* we ask, forgetting—or ignoring—that He is Lord of the universe.

Jonah had seen his nation's enemies coming to God. It didn't seem fair, and Jonah flew into a snit. In fact, he was so mad, he wanted to perish.

Anger often attacks when we feel helpless about our situation. We can't imagine things changing this way, and we hate it, so we want out. Death looks better than staying here and putting up with it.

But where would death have gotten the prophet? Would it have changed what God had done or helped Israel?

No.

We can lose ourselves in anger or trust that God is still good and still in control. After all, the changes of a day can't alter the truth of eternity.

Lord, I don't always understand the way You work, but I need to trust in You anyway. Help me to keep my eyes on You, not my own "should-be" plans.

August 16

"And that's not all," Haman added.
*"I'm the only person Queen Esther invited to
accompany the king to the banquet she gave.
And she has invited me along
with the king tomorrow."*
ESTHER 5:12

As proud Haman, King Xerxes' favored henchman, boasted to family and friends about his honors, he didn't know his downfall stood just around the corner.

Haman felt honored when the queen asked him to a banquet. But this was no celebration; it was her opportunity to report his perfidious actions to the king. Pride was deadly for Haman.

You've seen the damage pride causes on the job. A coworker gets a promotion, and before he has the new work under his belt, he's talking up his great achievements—until the day he's embarrassed as the boss uncovers all his mistakes. Or a good staff worker, jealous of a coworker, does everything she can to get her opponent out of her job—until the complainer is let go!

You're a valuable worker, but don't let pride blind you. Everyone can be replaced on the job.

When the blinders of pride surround me, Lord, open my eyes to Your truth. Clear my vision and my heart.

August 17

Catch for us the foxes,
the little foxes that ruin the vineyards,
our vineyards that are in bloom.
SONG OF SONGS 2:15

Leave your dirty dishes overnight, and what could have been an easy cleaning job becomes a crusty, dried-on mess. Don't do them in the morning, and their smell could soon drive you from your home.

Sin is like those dishes. Deal with it when you first notice it in your life, and it doesn't get ingrained. You confess it to God, turn away from it quickly, and like the little fox mentioned in Song of Songs, it won't become a big fox that ruins the fruit in your spiritual vineyard.

Ignore sin until it has a real hold on you, and your vines start dying.

Are you bearing a grudge, ignoring a task God has set before you, or losing sight of your daily walk with God? Act today. Move that little fox out of your spiritual life and into the forest, where it belongs.

Lord, I don't want sin growing in my life instead of Your fruit of the Spirit. Rid me of unforgiven sin.

August 18

Brothers, if someone is caught in a sin,
you who are spiritual should restore him gently.
But watch yourself, or you also may be tempted.
GALATIANS 6:1

When Elaine saw Freida getting romantically involved with a non-Christian, she felt concerned. Not that they were best friends or that the guy was a "bad" one, but she knew he didn't know Jesus and that Christians shouldn't get too involved with someone who didn't share their love for God.

So Elaine went to Treena and told her what was happening. But that wasn't enough. Soon everyone at church heard Elaine's criticism. She just couldn't seem to stop talking about it.

Elaine started out with right feelings. Any Christian who sees another in spiritual danger should be concerned. But after that she didn't follow the scriptural pattern. Gossiping couldn't lead Freida in the right direction.

All of us sin. As we start heading down the wrong path, we don't need a broadcaster. We need someone to gently remind us of the Scriptures we already know and to support us in making hard decisions.

If we see sin in another, we need to help, not fall into our own sin.

Lord, I don't like correcting other people. Show me how to reach out to them in love and understanding, not criticism.

August 19

Then came the Jews round about him,
and said unto him. . . "If thou be the Christ,
tell us plainly." Jesus answered them, "I told
you, and ye believed not: the works that I do in
my Father's name, they bear witness of me. But
ye believe not, because ye are not of my sheep."
JOHN 10:24–26, KJV

Some confused Jews wanted Jesus to say, "I am the Messiah," because they thought it would end their doubts.

Though Jesus didn't say those words, He pointed out that you know a person by what he or she does.

Jesus had taught in the streets and countryside, lived out in the open, and healed publicly. People saw who He was and what He did. Whether or not they liked it was another matter.

We live out our Christian testimony publicly, too. We can't act like Goody Two-shoes in church but commit sin privately and not have it subtly destroy our witness.

An honest testimony may convict unbelievers —or they may remain unconverted because of unbelief. Jesus didn't convince everyone He spoke to, and neither will we.

We're open witnesses, not conscience keepers.

Lord Jesus, I want my public testimony to reflect my private faith. Today I want people to see what You can do in my life.

August 20

Anyone who listens to the word
but does not do what it says is like a man
who looks at his face in a mirror and,
after looking at himself, goes away
and immediately forgets what he looks like.
JAMES 1:23–24

Scripture gives us a mirror-image picture of ourselves. Sometimes, when that view's sin-filled, we'd like to smash the mirror that shows us our true selves.

Those hard-to-face-up-to Bible passages show us our sin. We know we need to change our ways and struggle with that need. So we read the Word, even talk about it with other Christians, verbally agree to what it says, then turn our backs on it. We don't put the Word into action because we can't wait to lose our pain.

James compares turning our backs to forgetting what we look like. Disregarding the sin doesn't change our "face." God sees it, other people perceive it. We only fool ourselves.

When you see sin in the mirror, turn to God for forgiveness and healing. Only He can give you a new "face."

I'd rather walk a thousand miles than face up to sin, Lord. But start me on the pilgrimage that makes me clean and fit for You.

August 21

We all stumble in many ways.
If anyone is never at fault in what he says,
he is a perfect man, able to keep
his whole body in check.
JAMES 3:2

Can you imagine never saying the wrong thing? Never telling even the whitest of lies? Not embarrassing someone by saying something clumsy? Teaching the Word and getting everything right?

Life would be just about perfect if you could get your tongue under control.

That's what Scripture says. You see, what you say reflects all the things you're thinking and feeling. It shows who you really are.

Maybe we Christians have less trouble with our mouths than a coworker who swears constantly or someone who has low self-esteem and always berates herself. But *perfect?*

Only Jesus is truly perfect. He never put His foot in His mouth, gave bad advice, or unintentionally hurt someone. Sometimes He told the painful truth as a warning to sinners, but He was never mean.

Need to know what to say or how to say it? Look toward Jesus. Though you may still make mistakes, you'll draw closer to His contagious perfection every day.

O Perfect One, I want to be nearby, to catch more of Your nature every day.

August 22

*Then the LORD opened the donkey's mouth,
and she said to Balaam,
"What have I done to you to make you
beat me these three times?"*
NUMBERS 22:28

Balaam was made a donkey of by his own beast.

Approached by Balak, the king of Moab, Balaam was willing to curse the Israelites, who threatened Moab. But God clearly told the prophet not to do it.

When Balak enticed Balaam with a reward, Balaam hedged his bets by deciding to ask the Lord for clarification of His already clear orders. Then he decided to visit the king.

Heading toward Moab, Balaam had an eye-opening experience. His donkey balked at the sight of an angel. The angel-blind prophet still wanted to pass, and beat the animal, so the donkey started complaining out loud—in Balaam's own language!

What a fool Balaam must have felt. And he *was* a fool for questioning God.

Want Balaam's reputation? Question God when He tells you what church to go to, when not to take a job (or take one), and whom to marry. Doubt Him at every turn.

If you want to be a donkey, fine.

Lord, I don't want to make Balaam's mistake. Open my heart to Your directions. I want to obey.

August 23

*Thou, O LORD, remainest for ever; thy throne
from generation to generation.*
LAMENTATIONS 5:19, KJV

For verses, Jeremiah's been crying the blues about the destruction of Jerusalem. How can he suddenly write something like this?

Judah's situation was about as bad as it could get. Conquered by Babylon, Jeremiah's nation had been wiped out, her best people carted off into exile. Those who hadn't been killed or carried away were scrounging for food.

Pretty grim.

The prophet felt despondent, but he still knew whom he could turn to. God was their only hope, even if He took His time answering Jeremiah's prayer.

Sometimes life gets hopeless. The person you thought you'd marry says good-bye. A family member is dangerously ill. The job you thought you'd done so well at disappears.

But you still have hope. His name is Jesus, and He'll answer your prayers right on schedule.

Lord, when You don't answer my prayers the way I want, help me to keep trusting in You. What else can give me hope when life looks grim?

August 24

When neither sun nor stars appeared
for many days and the storm continued raging,
we finally gave up all hope of being saved.
ACTS 27:20

If you've ever been in a dangerous situation on a boat, you can understand the fears of Paul and his fellow travelers.

At sea, you can't just pull to the side of the road, get out, and call a tow truck. Winds and tide control your well-being. When the "road conditions" get bad, you can't get out and walk.

For three days Paul and his companions had been pushed around the Mediterranean Sea. Finally, exhausted emotionally and mentally, they gave up hope. Death seemed likely.

Even landlubbers can relate to Paul's feelings. In your Christian walk, haven't powerful forces threatened you? Your health, happiness, or spiritual well-being seemed endangered, and you couldn't stop the destruction. You couldn't pull over to the side of the road, either.

Paul and his friends didn't die. God protected them through a shipwreck.

He protects you, too. Just follow His road map.

Wherever my spiritual journey leads, I know I can count on You, Lord. Though storms blow, You'll never desert me.

August 25

Before certain men came from James, he [Peter] used to eat with the Gentiles. But when they arrived, he began to draw back and separate himself from the Gentiles because he was afraid of those who belonged to the circumcision group.
GALATIANS 2:12

Paul had a problem with brother Peter. Peter had taken a stand for the Gentiles, but when that stand seemed unpopular, he backed down.

Probably, Paul's irritation partly stemmed from his soft spot for the Gentiles, but even more, the apostle was upset at Peter's misunderstanding of the gospel. Faith in Jesus mattered, not rules and regulations.

Unlike many Christians, Paul didn't pass his displeasure on to the rest of the church first. He simply confronted Peter. This may not have been the first time they'd discussed the issue, since other Christians were on hand to hear them out.

When you disagree with a church member, do you follow Paul's plan for resolution? Or do you talk to everyone *except* the offender?

Paul and Peter's serious division would influence all Christianity, not just themselves. But they worked it out in love. You can do it, too.

Lord, I want to resolve conflict in the church, not add to it. Give me the courage to gently confront the one I disagree with.

August 26

Wounds from a friend can be trusted,
but an enemy multiplies kisses.
PROVERBS 27:6

For the first time, Shannon had begun to make a number of older friends. On the job, she found age often didn't matter as much as it had in school.

One day, Joan came to her with a criticism of her work.

"I thought she was my friend," Shannon mourned. "She's not even my boss! She may have been here for years, but she's at my level. How can she complain about my work?"

"Joan's not trying to hurt you," Carrie, another coworker, pointed out. "She didn't tell your boss about the mistake because she wanted to give you a chance to correct it. She's a good friend—don't take your feelings out on her."

In the office, some people talk as if they're your best friends but can't wait to stab you in the back. Others may correct you, hoping to help. A real friend wants the best for you. Take that correction, use it, and improve your career.

You have a *real* friend.

Thank You, Jesus, for the temporary hurts of a friend who helps me grow. Help me appreciate a love that shows itself in action.

August 27

In a single century we've gone from horse-and-buggy days to outer space. What scientific progress we've made.

But even the greatest scientific discovery hasn't found a cure for pride. If anything, our age of discovery has fueled our own arrogance. It's not uncommon for late twentieth-century people to look down on those from long ago. *How much more we know,* we think. *How ignorant they were.*

Such thinking disregards the fact that ancient Egyptians built pyramids using sophisticated techniques we can only guess at. People back then weren't so dumb.

Is it so hard to believe that the Messiah described by David, Isaiah, and other prophets could be real? These men weren't stupid, either; they just lived in a different time.

When people try to tell you the Bible can't be true, that its writers lived too long ago to know anything, understand that you're listening to human pride.

Turn to Jesus for the truth instead.

Lord, I don't want to get bound up in pride. Show me the light of Your truth.

August 28

Because I have sinned against him,
I will bear the LORD's wrath, until he
pleads my case and establishes my right.
He will bring me out into the light;
I will see his righteousness.
MICAH 7:9

Suppose a friend had a serious lawsuit against you. Can you imagine the case coming to trial and having that friend get up to plead your case?

It hardly seems possible. When a person has been harmed, the offender should pay a price—in money, time spent in jail, or retribution. If the plaintiff pleads for the defendant, it's as if he were asking for more pain.

But what if the plaintiff held the ultimate justice and was giving you a second chance? What if he knew that, in the end, right would be done, and he gave you another opportunity? That would seem fair, wouldn't it?

That's just what God does for you—He gives you another chance when you've sinned. Instead of taking pleasure in retribution, He wants to bring you into His righteousness. To make that possible, He gave His life for you.

Do you want retribution or forgiveness at work in your life?

Jesus, You'd have every right to punish me. Thank You for Your compassion that makes me holy instead. I need Your forgiveness today.

August 29

He forgave us all our sins,
having canceled the written code,
with its regulations, that was against us
and that stood opposed to us;
he took it away, nailing it to the cross.
COLOSSIANS 2:13–14

Credit card bills can be such stinkers—especially if you watch them skyrocket. Pay only the minimum balance, and that debt is yours forever.

What if you got a call from your credit card company one day saying, "Because you're our customer, we're canceling all your debt. We felt compassionate today"?

You'd probably go to a doctor to get your hearing checked. Or a psychiatrist to see if you were all right from the neck up. People don't just forgive business debts.

Paul describes sin as a business debt, with strict rules and regulations about payment and penalties.

On the cross, Jesus paid your ever-increasing debt and fulfilled those rules and regulations. At the same time He paid a perfect price for a valueless object—sin.

He did that because He loves you.

Can you ever feel valueless again?

Lord, You gave Your life for all my empty sin and made my life valuable again. Thank You for such love.

August 30

"For the Son of Man is going to come in his Father's glory with his angels, and then he will reward each person according to what he has done."
MATTHEW 16:27

My father can beat your father!" The words of a childish bully, pitting his dad against all comers, are usually pretty empty. Chances are, his dad wouldn't see the importance of the fight his son is setting up for him. The claim is only based on the son's need to feel he has the biggest and best dad.

By the time we hit our teens, we know Dad's strengths and weaknesses. We understand that he won't take on a classmate's dad unless there's a good reason. Even then, he won't do it physically, and he may not win.

But the Father Jesus describes isn't a bully and really can take on the whole world. They are so at one that the Son won't make a false claim for the Father.

Jesus isn't trying to bully the schoolyard. He's warning sinners of judgment to come.

Are your works and your soul ready for His reappearance?

Father God, I know You're no bully. I want to be ready when Your Son comes in glory. Hallelujah!

August 31

But Thomas, one of the twelve,
called Didymus. . .said unto them,
"Except I shall see in his hands the print of the
nails, and put my finger into the print of
the nails, and thrust my hands into his side,
I will not believe."
JOHN 20:24–25, KJV

How hard it must have been for Thomas Didymus, the Twin. Inside his mind, he had two poles. One said faith, the other, reason. No matter what the issue, he was pulled from side to side.

When the disciples told him they'd seen Jesus, Thomas sided with reason. Though he knew Peter, John, and the others weren't the lying sort, their report seemed unbelievable. Giving it credence would take a lot of blind faith, and Thomas wasn't going to be blind.

Thomas finally ended his battle between faith and reason with the words, "My Lord and my God" (v. 28), but only after seeing was believing. Reason had to be balanced equally with faith until Thomas saw Jesus and recognized Him as God.

Are you waiting to see things God wants you to trust by faith? You'll be missing the blessing of faith.

Jesus, I don't want a divided faith. Make me whole and strong in belief in You today.

September 1

*Rejoice in the LORD your God,
for he has given you the autumn rains
in righteousness. He sends you
abundant showers, both autumn and
spring rains, as before.*
JOEL 2:23

Most of us can stay dry if we want to. It's a luxury a lot of people don't have, though. And although a drought will raise supermarket prices, few of us will ever face starvation. We can pretty much avoid the downside of the weather nowadays.

Fortunately, God is good with the details of life. We don't really care if it rains on a given day or not, but He knows better and faithfully provides rain when it's needed. It's such a little detail to us that you'd think He would delegate it to someone else, but He hangs on to the responsibility and takes care of it for us. If He's faithful in this matter, imagine how faithful He is in everything else.

Father, thank You for the rain that falls and keeps the world in bloom. Only You know how all the parts of this world fit together and how to make it work the way You designed it.

September 2

Hope deferred makes the heart sick,
but a longing fulfilled is a tree of life.
PROVERBS 13:12

J ust when things seem to be going well, life can knock the pins out from under us and leave us watching our dreams fade away. Maybe you thought you'd finally found the right person to spend your life with, only to learn that your hope for love and marriage wasn't going to be fulfilled by that particular person.

It breaks your heart so badly that you give up for a while. Casual dating is safer, less painful. You back away from your hope, put it on the back burner, but it's still there, because once you've imagined a dream, it's impossible to let it go.

Eventually you'll risk loving again, and eventually you'll find the person you've been looking for—someone who shares your dream and makes it come true. Then everything will be brand-new and possible for you. You will be a new person, starting a new life with the one who fulfilled your dream.

Father, I know I will have to defer some of my hopes until it's time for them to be fulfilled. Don't let me give up on my dreams too soon, because I know You have great plans for me.

September 3

Good deeds are obvious,
and even those that are not cannot be hidden.
1 TIMOTHY 5:25

Some of our good deeds are obvious to everyone. If you regularly show up to do volunteer work, you will develop a reputation as a faithful worker. If you treat your parents with respect, the neighborhood will call you a good son or daughter. You don't do these things to impress others, but it's nice to be recognized as a good person.

Many of your good deeds will not be noticed by others, however, and you won't receive any praise for doing them. In fact, some may gain you nothing but trouble.

But that doesn't mean you should give up. Your concern and care may not be noticed or trusted, but God sees and remembers every good deed you do.

Father, it's hard to be distrusted when I know I am just trying to help. Sometimes I'm tempted to be as cynical as everyone else. When I'm hurt by someone's response to my good intentions, reassure me that I'm behaving the way You want me to.

September 4

"Blessed are the peacemakers:
for they shall be called the children of God."
MATTHEW 5:9, KJV

Have you ever found yourself in the middle of a family argument? Maybe your dad and brother are at odds over some issue, and you step in to try to bring them back together. You offer what you think is a reasonable compromise, only to have both of them tell you to butt out and mind your own business. Often the two of them will join forces and turn on you. Well, that's one problem solved—and another begun.

The problem with being a peacemaker is that you can't totally please both sides. They don't want to come to an agreement; they want to win! So what do you do, give up? Let them fight it out on their own? In some cases, you can do just that, but in others the stakes are too high, and you'll just have to accept the fact that both sides may end up hating you for the time being when you try to be a peacemaker. It isn't easy being a child of God.

Father, give me the courage to be a peacemaker when I can help and the good sense to know when my efforts will be useless. I want to do Your will, whatever the cost.

September 5

*"Let your light shine before men,
that they may see your good deeds
and praise your Father in heaven."*
MATTHEW 5:16

If you are going to do good deeds, it's a good idea to be sure of your motivation. Are you secretly doing them for your own reputation or pleasure, or are you doing them for the glory of God?

Although doing good deeds involves action on your part, the greater portion of them also involves inaction. A light doesn't shine for its own glory. It just sits there and glows, showing the actions of others, just like a mirror doesn't physically do anything but reflect the actions of others.

In the same way, good deeds should show and reflect the actions of God, not you. It's God who gives you the motivation to do good. Even if others see you doing the acts, what they should notice is God's love, not yours. This makes doing a simple good deed a little more complicated than you thought, but eventually you'll catch on and learn to reflect God while you stand back in the shadows.

Lord, I want my actions to lead others to praise You, not me. Show me how to do this in my everyday life.

September 6

Do not pollute the land where you are.
NUMBERS 35:33

In this verse the Bible is talking about how letting people get away with murder pollutes a country, but we all know that other actions or inactions pollute, too. Injustice, greed, and exploitation of any resource can be a source of pollution, making the land unfit for habitation.

We humans are the only species that fouls its own nest. In nature, one animal cleans up after another, whether it's a mother bird throwing dirty nesting material out of her nest or a jackal cleaning up after a lion's feast. What one animal wastes is ultimately used by another.

The problem is, we pollute on such a grand scale that nature can't keep up with us. One dumped car in a creek will eventually rust away and be used as a fish shelter, but twenty of them will choke off the stream and flood the land above it. Everything in nature is self-cleaning, except for us.

Father, remind me that my little thoughtless acts of pollution can amount to disaster for another species that You created. Teach me how to live in harmony with all of Your creation.

September 7

*Continue in what you have learned
and have become convinced of,
because you know those from
whom you learned it.*
2 TIMOTHY 3:14

It's always a good idea to know who is teaching you what. A lot of us learn from the media. Modern communication is a wonderful tool, but do you know what the commentator believes and how that may influence him to skew his report one way or another? Do you take the time to really look into issues for yourself, or do you just take someone's word for what's going on?

Before you swallow something whole, look at it carefully. Does it agree with what you believe in? Have teachers you trust said the same thing about this issue? Can you see a hidden agenda there that someone hopes you will miss? Until proven otherwise, it's a good idea to trust your old, familiar teachers instead of those you do not know at all.

Father, teach me discernment in what I believe and trust in. I need to learn to make up my own mind, not blindly follow the leading of others.

September 8

*Blessed shalt thou be in the city,
and blessed shalt thou be in the field.*
DEUTERONOMY 28:3, KJV

People get locked into mental mind-sets that can strongly affect the way they look at life. Those who live in great cities consider anyone living elsewhere as hicks, narrow-minded, and somewhat slow both physically and mentally. Those living in small towns think all city dwellers are heartless, cold, and narrow-minded. City folk transformed into country folk say they are never accepted in their new homes, while those who move from the country to the city say the exact same thing.

Nothing is ever going to change this. We can always find someone to look down on, and even though the Bible warns us not to act this way, it still goes on.

What we continue to forget is that God really doesn't care where we live. To Him, it's how we live that counts, and we can live a blessed life anywhere we want to. Good people can live in cities or towns; bad people can live on farms or in condos. It's not the place that counts, it's the hearts living there.

Father, teach me not to judge people on the basis of where they live, but accept everyone as a potential child of God.

September 9

*Of making many books there is no end,
and much study wearies the body.*
ECCLESIASTES 12:12

If you are starting some night classes this month, you'll soon understand this verse all too well. School bookstores are all stocked up, waiting for you to fill your arms and empty your wallets on textbooks, each costing more than a good meal for two at a restaurant with tablecloths.

The sticker shock is bad enough, but after you stack your books on your desk, it will suddenly dawn on you that over the next few months you will actually be expected to *read* them all! Not only will you read them, you will have to remember what you've read. The sheer volume of pages waiting for you is intimidating. Just thinking about it wearies the body. How will you ever find the time?

Well, don't lose faith in yourself. You've done it before, remember? And God will be with you to help you.

Father, more education is exciting, but a little frightening, too. Stay by my side in the next few weeks as I get used to my new responsibilities.

September 10

Make it your ambition to lead a quiet life,
to mind your own business
and to work with your hands. . .
so that your daily life may win the respect
of outsiders and so that you will not be
dependent on anybody.
1 THESSALONIANS 4:11–12

These verses summarize the aim of all education: to be able to take care of yourself when you go out into the world. They also tell you how to act when you're supporting yourself while furthering your education: Lead a quiet life, mind your own business, and do your work.

Assignments, term papers, and demanding teachers will pretty much see to it that you lead a quiet life—relatively speaking, that is. If you're trying to balance work while getting a higher degree, you need to strike a delicate balance between work and relaxation. One way or another, the work has to get done, but you do need to take time for fun. This is a balance you need to find with God's help.

Father, help me figure out how to get everything done and still have some time to enjoy myself.

September 11

*Even in laughter the heart may ache,
and joy may end in grief.*
PROVERBS 14:13

You probably know the story of the clown who managed to keep on laughing although his heart was breaking. He had a job to do, no matter how he felt personally, so he did it. Depending on your point of view, you can think of that clown as a hero or a fool, but either way he put others before himself.

Laughter and tears are close relatives. We can laugh so hard it brings tears to our eyes, and sometimes we find ourselves laughing in an unconscious attempt to cope with intense sorrow. More than a few people have been struck with the giggles during a funeral. It's embarrassing and inappropriate, but it's just another human reaction to grief.

We can never predict how someone will handle strong emotions, and we certainly should not judge anyone on the basis of how they handle their emotions under stress.

Father, I realize not everyone has a firm grip on their emotions and I should never be too hasty to condemn someone's reaction to a stressful event. Help me give the support that is needed, whether it's tears or laughter.

September 12

Plans succeed through good counsel.
PROVERBS 20:18, NLT

If you've graduated last spring, you've probably had all the advice you want for a while. Parents, grandparents, teachers, pastors, and guidance counselors have been telling you what to do for the last twenty years. It's time for you to make your own plans.

You're right. You probably are ready to do your own thing. No one wants you to come running for help with every little decision. You have to make your own choices and live with the results.

That doesn't mean you won't still want some selective advice, though. This time you will seek it out, instead of having others determine what you need to know. The initiative is yours now. If you have a little money to invest, you can find your own financial advisor. A friend can tell you about a good doctor or dentist. A mentor at work can advise you on how to get ahead. The advice you seek out yourself can be even more valuable than the advice someone pushes on you without asking if you want it.

Father, help me find the advice I need to make my plans work out. I don't know everything, and I do need to know the questions I should be asking.

September 13

[Love] *always protects, always trusts,
always hopes, always perseveres.*
1 CORINTHIANS 13:7

Wouldn't it be great to find love like that in another human being? Especially the *always* part? Human love often comes up short of always. Sometimes it doesn't protect, trust, hope, and persevere, either. Since people aren't perfect, it's unreasonable to expect perfect human love.

Still, that's what we hope to find, and some of our early relationships fall apart when we spot signs of imperfection. Eventually we learn not to expect so much, lower our standards here and there, and find someone who's close enough. After all, we're not perfect, either, and learning to adjust is necessary in all things human.

The only place we'll ever find perfect love is in God's love for us, which never disappoints or fails. When our human love becomes a little ragged around the edges, we need to follow the model God provides, protecting, trusting, hoping, and persevering over everything until our love becomes as perfect as we can make it.

Father, our love should be a small reflection of Your love. Though I know it will never be perfect, I will give it my all.

September 14

Cast all your anxiety on him
because he cares for you.
1 PETER 5:7

Have you discovered the difference between fear and anxiety yet? They're not the same. For one thing, fear is productive. Fear is that heart-thumping moment when you know it could all be over. The car that appears over the hill while you're passing another car causes a stab of fear, which in turn gets you back into the right-hand lane as fast as possible. Fear can be dealt with by an action you can take. Most of the time, fear helps you save yourself.

Anxiety is never productive. There is no immediate danger in sight, just a vague, overpowering feeling of impending disaster. Anxiety over car accidents may keep you out of cars, but it never teaches you to be a good driver. Anxiety paralyzes you, takes you out of the action altogether. It's a useless emotion that cripples a perfectly good life.

The Bible tells us to shun anxiety, to throw it all on God. There's enough in the world that deserves our fear, but nothing in the world should make us anxious.

Father, when anxiety takes hold of me and paralyzes me, teach me to give it over to You.

September 15

*Apply your heart to instruction
and your ears to words of knowledge.*
PROVERBS 23:12

Everyone looks back on high school and college days as days of carefree fun. Of course that's because additional cares and responsibilities follow the school years, and sometimes catching the 7:00 A.M. train makes sitting in a classroom seem a piece of cake.

The truth is, learning is hard work. It's not half as carefree as we remember it being. Names, dates, equations, philosophies, term papers, and unreasonably high grade curves give students a lot of grief. All that knowledge doesn't just flow into your brain and stick. If you're juggling coursework for a higher degree with work responsibilities, you're probably realizing that fact all over again.

Don't be discouraged, though. No matter what challenges life brings you, your heavenly Father is always by your side, waiting to help you out.

Father, remind me today that nothing is too hard for me when You are by my side.

September 16

The eternal God is thy refuge,
and underneath are the everlasting arms.
DEUTERONOMY 33:27, KJV

Sometimes we think of God as an avenger, punisher, and slayer of the unrighteous—someone we'd better not cross. The Old Testament, read too hastily, often gives us that idea, with all its curses, fires, destroyed nations.

And yet, right there in Deuteronomy is this verse, with its loving promise. God is also our refuge, the one we can always run to. He protects us from bullies, just like our big brother did. He kisses our wounds and makes them better, like Mom. He opens His arms—His *everlasting* arms—and protects us from those who would hurt us, just like Dad.

Whenever we're far from home, struggling to make our way in a cutthroat world, God will be there for us. He's never too busy to help. His lap is never too full for one more lost kid. He never fails to comfort and protect.

We don't deserve this much love. We can't even begin to imagine it. And yet it's there for us anytime we need it.

Father, thank You for letting me climb into Your everlasting arms anytime I need to, for saving my life anytime it needs it, for being my Father.

September 17

A righteous man may have many troubles,
but the LORD delivers him from them all.
PSALM 34:19

Being righteous is no guarantee of a trouble-free life. As long as we're human, we'll have problems, whether we bring them on ourselves or have them thrust upon us. In addition to poverty, wars, and famine, lots of other problems can bring us down.

If we are righteous, God promises to deliver us from all our problems, but He does it His way, in His time, and we usually get a little impatient. Some of our troubles never seem to leave us. We may even die surrounded by them, waiting to our last breath to be delivered from them. Has God forgotten us? Why are we still suffering?

We don't know why or when or how. We just don't know. We can't see into the mind of God; we can't imagine His plans. We might not even recognize His deliverance when it does come. All we can do is trust Him and know He never fails to keep His promises. But He never promised we'd totally understand in this lifetime.

Father, when troubles surround me, help me trust in Your promises and never give up hope.

September 18

For he will command his angels concerning
you to guard you in all your ways;
they will lift you up in their hands, so that you
will not strike your foot against a stone.
PSALM 91:11–12

Your mother or grandmother probably told you about your guardian angel when you were young and afraid to look under your bed at night, but did he fade away after the great Santa Claus debacle?

Some people have great confidence in the protection of angels, while others consign them to the "wouldn't that be nice?" category. And yet the Bible tells us that angels play a very active role in our lives, guarding us in *all* our ways. They even pick us up with their hands when we're in danger of stubbing our toes on a tiny little stone we never see. If a simple walk around the block requires angelic assistance, imagine how much work must go into a whole life!

Of course we have to remember not to make idols of the angels, who are only obeying the commands of God concerning us. Still, it's nice to have them around.

Father, thank You for the protection of the angels You have assigned to my care. I may never be conscious of them in my life, but I know they are there, doing Your will for my benefit.

September 19

*"If anyone is ashamed of me and my words,
the Son of Man will be ashamed of him."*
LUKE 9:26

It's not that we're ashamed of God or His words, but sometimes we are a little embarrassed by the actions required of us when we believe. Some people have no problem with saying grace in a crowded restaurant; others hope Grandpa will keep it down a little. As far as witnessing goes, we may stumble through it, but we seldom go looking for the opportunity.

Fortunately, the tongue-tied among us have other ways of showing God's love to others. We do it when we give God credit for our successes, live our lives in a godly manner, practice justice, and show humility. All of these are well within our reach, even if the thought of face-to-face witnessing drives our blood pressure through the roof. God knows we have differing talents and abilities and expects us to use them for His glory. As we draw closer to Him, our tongues may even loosen up and we'll realize that we weren't ashamed at all, just too worried about others' opinions.

Father, please accept my stumbling attempts to give praise to You and understand that I am doing the best I can. Others do this far better, but my heart is in the right place.

September 20

*Little children,
let no man deceive you.*
1 JOHN 3:7, KJV

It's easy enough to go astray with no help at all. At least then we only have ourselves to blame. But it gets more complicated when others are involved. Is your roommate to blame when the two of you go out for a night on the town and you overdo it? Did he lead you astray, or did you follow along with no encouragement at all?

There are plenty of people out there willing and able to lead you off in the wrong direction. Indeed, finding someone who wants to lead you in the right direction is pretty hard. But who is truly responsible when you fall? Certainly not God, and probably no other human being. The verse above says do not *let* anyone lead you astray. There's a choice involved, and it's up to you to make the final decision.

Father, give me the courage not to be a blind follower of others. Instead, help me see where others are heading, so I can get off the wrong path in time and follow Your way.

September 21

For our backsliding is great;
we have sinned against you.
JEREMIAH 14:7

Choosing the moral way certainly leads to an interesting life. One day you feel that you've got it down pat. You know where you're going and are zipping right along on the highway to heaven. The next day, you're up to your axles in mud, going nowhere at all or being towed back to some intersection you passed years ago.

Backsliding is a devastating experience. You'd licked that problem. There were plenty of others to work on, but that particular one was behind you forever (you thought). But there it is again, standing in the middle of the road and mocking you. Maybe it'll be easier to get past it this time, but what a waste of effort.

Even when we know that God has forgiven our sins, we still get ticked off at our failures. They hurt our egos. When we backslide, however, the only thing we can do is confess our failure, accept God's forgiveness, and get back on the road again. It's a long journey, and there's no point in wallowing in the mud.

Father, thank You for Your forgiveness when I lose my way. I can never be the person I want to be without Your help and encouragement.

September 22

*A gossip betrays a confidence;
so avoid a man who talks too much.*
PROVERBS 20:19

Have you noticed that the more you talk, the greater the chance that you'll goof things up? You say the wrong thing to the wrong person, including some things you never meant to say at all. We often do this when we're under pressure of some kind. To avoid seeming stuck up, we say the first thing that comes to mind, only to hear ourselves talking about some deep, dark secret we weren't supposed to know about. To fit in with the crowd, we often say things we know are untrue or improper. Our tongues are in overdrive, but our brains are on hold.

Fear does this to us—fear of being left out, of being thought stupid. We feel that if we talk fast enough, others will overlook our faults and be lulled into acceptance by our silver tongues, so we let the words tumble out, only to find we've sabotaged ourselves.

The next time you feel pressured to blurt out a confidence, excuse yourself for a minute until the temptation passes. Two minutes of silence are worth far more than one minute of foolishness.

Father, teach me to guard my tongue when nervousness makes me want to ramble on.

September 23

Charm is deceptive,
and beauty is fleeting;
but a woman who fears the LORD
is to be praised.
PROVERBS 31:30

This verse applies equally to men and women and should always be kept in mind during the dating years. Sure, everyone wants to date charming, beautiful people. Even those who are less than charming or beautiful themselves hope to connect with someone who qualifies.

But you can't choose a spouse on the basis of charm and looks alone. Neither can you rule out others on the basis of a lack of charm and beauty. Take a long, hard look in the mirror and then picture what you will look like in ten or twenty years. Don't you still hope to find someone to love the real you? Can you expect this from others and not give it to them in return?

Charm and beauty are simply attractants. Their job is to get someone's attention and give you the chance to win them. They're like the beautiful flower that makes it possible for a plant to reproduce, then fades away. It's the whole plant that's important, not just the flower.

Father, teach me to look beyond the surface and fall in love with a whole person, not just a pretty face.

September 24

The borrower is servant to the lender.
PROVERBS 22:7, KJV

It takes twelve years' work to graduate from high school or sixteen to get through college. That's years of books and papers, thousands of dollars invested in clothing, transportation, housing, and tuition. A diploma represents untaken vacations, overtime work, rent payments, and meals of hot dogs and beans instead of steak.

Did everyone go through all this so you could end up as someone's servant? But that's exactly what you will be if you grab your first credit card and pile on the fun. Who gets the first crack at your paycheck? The credit card people. They have to be paid first, month after month. It's a job you can't leave behind you—a servant's job. If your credit bill is high enough, you won't even be able to tithe, let alone save.

One credit card may be necessary for emergency use, but more than one only leads to disaster at this point in your life. You're a graduate, not a slave, so take control of your own life by taking control of your expenses.

Father, teach me how to live on what I make, not on my credit card limit. I don't need to be a servant to anyone but You.

September 25

*When I called, you answered me;
you made me bold and stouthearted.*
PSALM 138:3

David had a close, intimate relationship with God. When David did wrong, God did not hesitate to punish him, even harshly at times. When he did what was right, he was rewarded magnificently. This doesn't mean David had an easy life. His father-in-law pursued him in the wilderness for years, determined to kill him. Great armies attacked his kingdom through much of his reign, and his own beloved son stole his crown.

David didn't hesitate to complain to God when things were going badly, but through it all he made a point of celebrating and glorifying God's greatness. No matter what happened to him, David knew God was righteous and would answer his prayers, and this confidence made him strong.

That same confidence is available to you today. When you call on God, He will answer. He will make you bold and stouthearted. All you need to do is ask.

Father, thank You for being there for me when I call on You for help. Your help makes me strong and confident.

September 26

Those who are wise will shine
like the brightness of the heavens,
and those who lead many to righteousness,
like the stars for ever and ever.
DANIEL 12:3

Here Daniel is discussing Judgment Day, when everyone will receive his reward and some will shine like the stars forever. But even in our times, there are those who stand out with a certain steady radiance.

Most of them would deny it if you called them living saints. They'd be embarrassed by such a label because they know how far short they fall from being perfect, but saints don't have to be perfect. They do what they do without fanfare—quietly, humbly, faithfully.

You probably know one or two of these quiet saints. They come from all walks of life and live quietly, but their actions change lives. Look back on your life. Who changed it for the good just by being there for you? Who did you look up to as an example of goodness? What makes them shine for you?

Once you've identified these crucial people in your life, go and do likewise.

Father, thank You for all those who have served as godly examples for me. Now help me follow their example and try to do the same for others.

September 27

*If we are thrown into the blazing furnace,
the God we serve is able to save us from it,
and he will rescue us from your hand, O king.
But even if he does not, we want you to know,
O king, that we will not serve your gods
or worship the image of gold you have set up.*
DANIEL 3:17–18

Shadrach, Meshach, and Abednego didn't mess around, even when threatened by a king. Notice their tone of voice in these verses. They're polite, but they're sure not groveling.

Don't be fooled—we, too, are asked to worship idols every day. They aren't gold statues, and no one expects us to physically fall down before them, but they do influence our lives.

There's the idol of the bottom line that's worshipped by corporations. Mess with that one, and you're out of work. There's the idol of personal beauty that steals our time, effort, and money and urges us to admire the unadmirable. There's the idol of personal wealth that convinces us to work at jobs we hate and act more aggressively than we should.

What are your personal idols? Can you be as strong as Shadrach, Meshach, and Abednego and reject them?

Father, show me the idols of my heart and deliver me from them.

September 28

For we hear that there are some which
walk among you disorderly, working not at all,
but are busybodies. Now them that are such
we command and exhort by our Lord Jesus
Christ, that with quietness they work,
and eat their own bread.
2 THESSALONIANS 3:11–12, KJV

Some people get away without working. A lot of them are young, still living at home, and being supported by their parents until they "find themselves." Well, what they need to find is a job. *Any* job.

There will always be those who are legitimately unable to support themselves, but we're not talking about them. We're talking about those who can't earn what they think they "deserve," those who are above taking a minimum-wage job and working their way up a rung at a time. Others can't find a "fulfilling" job. Ask your grandparents if their jobs were fulfilling and give them a good laugh. Sometimes just putting bread on the table is fulfillment enough.

God gave most of us the basic equipment necessary to earn a living: two hands, a strong back, and a nimble brain. You're not going to start at the top, but until you start somewhere, you're going nowhere.

Father, thank You for giving me the ability to pro-
vide for myself. The rest is up to me now.

September 29

*Do not be carried away by
all kinds of strange teachings.*
HEBREWS 13:9

We're a curious species, always eager to look into something new and exciting. That's good. Without our urge to explore, we'd still be dropping like flies from diseases. Without transportation, our world would consist of the five- or ten-mile radius around our homes. We explore, learn, and improve.

As we do, we'll run into some pretty strange teachings. Some of them may prove worthy with time, but others will turn out to be shams or simple mistakes or misunderstandings. It's confusing. Look at the whole field of alternative medicine today. Some of its approaches may prove to be valid, while others will be foolishness. Right now, even traditional medicine keeps giving us contradictory advice: eat fish. . .no, don't; butter or margarine? Zinc for colds or vitamin C or chicken soup?

The best advice is found in the verse above: Don't get carried away with anything. Give time and experience the chance to clarify a new discovery before you wrap your life up in it. Be cautious of new teachings, but keep an open mind.

Father, knowledge is increasing faster than our brains can sort out fact from fiction. Give me a level head.

September 30

A righteous man is cautious in friendship.
PROVERBS 12:26

We need friends at all stages of our lives, but especially when we're young and still trying to figure life out. Friends give us other viewpoints to consider. When we share experiences, we can save ourselves a great deal of time by avoiding some of our friends' mistakes. We trust friends, often more than we trust our parents, because we have more in common with them.

Which is exactly why we need to be cautious in choosing our friends. Sometimes they betray us. Sometimes we discover they're not going in the direction we want to go, and it's hard to break up a friendship when we make this discovery.

Friendships also change as they mature, and sometimes these changes will hurt. Friends grow apart and then reconnect as time goes by, in a sort of cyclical flow—acquaintance, friend, acquaintance, friend again. A good friendship can tolerate these changes and grow stronger with each fluctuation. Choose your friends cautiously, and when you find a good one, hang onto him or her throughout your life.

Father, help me choose my friends with care and treasure those who stick by me through all life's ups and downs.

October 1

Leanne felt awful when she thought about the troubles her friend Maya had. She'd become a radiant Christian in college, but not long after, she had slid into unhappiness. Married a year after graduation, Maya was separated from her husband within months. From there, she got and lost jobs and never seemed to settle in to adult life.

Maya had been a Christian; of that Leanne was sure. What had happened to her friend?

Not until they got together for lunch one day did Leanne begin to discover the truth. Maya did know Christ, but she hadn't given her whole life up to Him. A few major areas were "off limits" to God.

"God's been dealing with me through all this. He's been cleaning out the closets and making me a *real* Christian. I just had to hurt enough to come back to Him."

God doesn't want to make a Christian miserable, but He'll do what He has to do to get our attention. After all, He loves His children so much, He wants each by His side.

Thank You, Father, for loving me enough to let nothing keep us apart.

October 2

*Nevertheless he saved them for his name's sake,
that he might make his mighty power
to be known*
PSALM 106:8, KJV

On their trip out of Egypt, the Israelites forgot God's miracles. They weren't even to the Promised Land, and already they were suffering from short-term memory loss!

Most of us could have understood if God had simply left this pigheaded people in the desert. "Find your own way!" each of us might have responded. "See if I care if you ever get out."

God isn't like that. When we disobey, He doesn't totally give up on us. But neither is His some wimpy compassion. He doesn't save us from our troubles just because, like a parent with a fussy child, He's tired of hearing our complaints.

The Lord of creation saves us to show the world what kind of stuff He's made of. How would anyone know what kind of God He is if He ignored our plight or constantly gave in to our whining? How would they know of His omnipotence?

He saves us because He's wonderful, not because we are.

Lord, thank You for loving me, even when I forget You. What a huge, glorious God You are!

October 3

*I long to see you so that I may impart to you
some spiritual gift to make you strong—
that is, that you and I may be mutually
encouraged by each other's faith.*
ROMANS 1:11–12

We think of Paul as a tough guy. After all, didn't he stand firm for his faith, even though it meant being stoned, imprisoned, and ridiculed? *Could we withstand all that?* we wonder. Paul must be a superman, right?

But in this verse we see a bit of Paul's vulnerable side. He didn't want to visit Rome to show off how great he was. He wanted to use his abilities to bless the Romans. But the powerful apostle also needed something from them—their encouragement.

Paul wasn't a stand-alone tough guy who set out to take on the world. Though God's Spirit made him powerful, he still needed other people to encourage and uplift him.

Even the spiritual "tough guys" among us have days when they just wish someone would tell them they're doing a great job or being a fantastic friend. You never know when that encouragement could help your pastor, youth leader, or friend.

Why not say that word to someone today?

Show me someone I can encourage today, Lord.

October 4

For the word of God is living and active.
Sharper than any double-edged sword,
it penetrates even to dividing soul
and spirit, joints and marrow; it judges
the thoughts and attitudes of the heart.
HEBREWS 4:12

Have you ever picked up your devotional, read the Scripture, and felt as if God had written that verse especially for you? It went right to your heart because you were living out that verse.

The Bible isn't like any other book. Though you might enjoy a novel or learn a lot from a how-to book, neither reaches deep inside your soul the way Scripture does. The Word of God gets straight inside you and cuts to the truth in an instant. The Spirit can wield it like a sword, cutting sin out of your life.

But you have to hold still while God uses that sword; otherwise you can get all cut up. You'll leave a painful quiet time without the benefit of having the cancer of sin removed. Let God have His way with you, and though the sword might hurt at first, healing can come rapidly.

By the end of your prayers, you might feel whole again.

Holy Spirit, reach into my life with Your Word. Search out the places where sin hides and remove it from my life.

October 5

Elijah was afraid and ran for his life.
1 Kings 19:3

In a showdown with the priests of Baal, Elijah flourished God's power in their faces, while they couldn't even seem to get their deity's attention. It was a great spiritual victory.

Just when Elijah was on top of the world, wicked Queen Jezebel threatened to kill him. Terrified, Elijah ran.

Why would anyone who had seen God's power fear this woman? Wasn't Elijah wrong to run? Curiously, Scripture doesn't say that. Instead, God merely sent an encouraging angel to give Elijah rest.

One great spiritual victory didn't make the prophet cocky. Elijah didn't assume that because God had used him to outdo the priests of Baal not even the queen could touch him. He didn't feel invincible, he felt tired. Elijah needed a rest, not another battle.

When God has done great things in your life, do you leap ahead into new battles without being certain this is where God wants you to be? Be as obedient as Elijah and seek Him first.

Lord, I want to do great things for You, but more than that I want to be in Your will. Give me wisdom about which battles I need to take on.

October 6

Oh, that thou wouldest. . .come down. . .
to make thy name known to thine adversaries,
that the nations may tremble at thy presence!
ISAIAH 64:1–2, KJV

When another nation takes a stand that, to us, is obviously against God's will, anger stirs our hearts. Like Isaiah, we may wish God would set the record straight in an act that would get the world's attention.

But before we ask God to wipe someone else out, we need to look at our own nation. No country made up of imperfect human beings will always do right. Thank God that mercy tempers His justice. Without that, we, too, would be wiped out.

God doesn't want us to ignore or excuse every wrong that happens in the world, but He doesn't want us just pointing the finger. Instead of setting ourselves up as critics, we need to reach out to individuals in need.

We can do that by encouraging our country to take right stands—whether it's at home or abroad. That way our nation can have a character pleasing to God.

Lord, I want to spread Your love to the world, but I need to start in my own neighborhood. Today, show me someone I can help.

October 7

*Man's anger does not bring about
the righteous life that God desires.*
JAMES 1:20

But don't I have to get all my anger in the open to get rid of it?" Jaquie asked. "I've always heard it isn't good to bottle it up. Besides, my family argues all the time. I wouldn't know what else to do."

If anger resides in your home, like Jaquie, you may feel baffled by this verse. You don't even know where to start.

Jaquie learned she had a choice: She could go to God with the problems that caused those emotions and deal with them before she opened her mouth, or she could batter others with the feelings that kept growing inside her.

Consistently bringing your hurts to Jesus first defuses the situation. He can show you what's really wrong and give insight on how to fix it. He can soothe painful emotions by bringing understanding to both sides.

Or you can let that anger burn, ever growing and destroying your life and those around you.

Get your anger out in the open—to God.

When I'm tempted to respond with anger, Lord, turn me instead to You.

October 8

*Do nothing out of selfish ambition or
vain conceit, but in humility consider
others better than yourselves.*
PHILIPPIANS 2:3

It took me a long time to figure out why Mom and Dad have such a happy marriage," Gail told her brother. "Finally I decided it's because they must have Philippians 2:3 as their watchword. They're so humble with each other."

Good marital relationships are founded on a kind of reciprocal-care agreement. Instead of looking out for personal interests and then considering the spouse, each partner of a successful couple puts aside selfishness and puts the other first. Neither gets cheated when *both* have that attitude.

One member doesn't constantly knuckle under to the other, fear offending the other, or give up every scrap of identity. None of those concepts fit Paul's description.

This verse isn't just for marriages. *Any* relationship becomes a blessing when people mutually care for each other. Imagine what churches would be like if Christians treated each other this way!

Whether it's another church member, a date, or a spouse, help me to put others first, Lord. I want to let them know they're loved.

October 9

Today, if you hear his voice,
do not harden your hearts as you did. . .
during the time of testing in the desert.
HEBREWS 3:7–8

I guess my spiritual walk is as good as any-one's," Tim said. "I mean, I don't think I have to live like a pastor or anything, but I know God saved me."

"What do you mean?" Karl asked.

"Well, I can still enjoy myself, you know. All those rules in the Bible are really just for pastors."

Karl had never known that Tim's commitment level was so low. A serious Christian walk isn't something just for "professional Christians"—church leaders who get paid for their work. God calls every Christian to listen to Him every day.

Close your ears to Him, and like Tim, your heart starts to harden. Before long, you don't even realize how far you've strayed.

Open your heart to Him, and the gentle rains of the Spirit turn your life into a verdant garden.

Lord, I don't want to spend a lifetime in the desert when I can live in a garden. Show me today how I can do Your will.

October 10

Life is so precious that not even the most wealthy person in the world could pay its real worth. Gold, paper bills, or any other financial system man has developed just can't compare to the value God places on a human being.

The Bible only speaks of One who can pay the high ransom: Jesus (Matthew 20:28). Because He was not just a man, but also God, He could pay the price. Just think. You are so valuable to God that even if someone offered Him all the wealth of the world, He would turn them down. God took only the very best for you—Jesus.

The next time someone tries to tell you you're worthless, turn to this psalm. Remember that One greater than your critic says just the opposite, and He paid the price with His Son.

Lord, the world is always telling me I'm not worth much. Thank You for loving me more than the entire world.

October 11

Make sure that nobody
pays back wrong for wrong,
but always try to be kind to
each other and to everyone else.
1 THESSALONIANS 5:15

But you don't know what he did to me!" or, "You don't know how she hurt me!" How often people say or think these words as justification for getting back at someone who hurt them badly. The implication always follows that they have a right to retaliate. Our desire to even the score runs strong when we've been done wrong.

But it isn't the best way. When we seek our own justice, we forget how it pales before God's justice. If we leave wrongs in His hands, pray for our abusers, and wait, wonderful things can happen.

Instead of starting a long-term feud, make peace with your enemy. He may turn into a friend. But if God brings down His own justice, it will be better than yours ever could be.

Be kind to those who hurt you. Either way, you can't lose.

Father God, thank You that Your justice is far greater than mine. When I'm wronged, let me leave the outcome of the situation in Your hands.

October 12

*For we know that our old self
was crucified with him. . .
that we should no longer be slaves to sin.*
ROMANS 6:6

Giving up that old pair of sneakers is hard. Though you buy a new pair, for a while the old favorites hang around in the back of your closet and get used when you need to feel comfy.

Being a brand-new Christian can feel like those sneakers. The life before Christ still feels more comfortable. In those B.C. days, life wasn't so challenging. Snug in sin, you didn't change much. God wasn't pulling at your heart.

Let sin stay at the back of your closet, though, and you're denying the work God has already done in you. He says you're no longer a slave to sin. You don't *have* to give in when you feel it lurking.

Keeping the old temptations in your living space means sin will still creep in. Give in to sin, and except for the ache in your heart, you'll feel as if Jesus never saved you at all. Why be a slave, when God set you free?

Lord, cleanse me from my old life and fill me with Your sparkling new one.

October 13

May the peoples praise you, O God. . . .
Then the land will yield its harvest,
and God, our God, will bless us.
PSALM 67:5–6

What does praise have to do with a good harvest?

Unlike the Israelites, you may not go out to a field every day to earn your living. But that doesn't mean these verses don't apply to you. The principle that as a nation our physical blessings can never exceed our spiritual blessings still works.

Worship for God shouldn't be a separate cubbyhole, completely apart from our work lives. Our spiritual attitudes spill over into the things we do every day. When we have great relationships with God, we do better at our jobs, deal better with our coworkers, and truly aid people.

The nation that worships God and tells others of His wonders will be blessed. Suddenly the country's economy takes a turn for the better, because people are being honest with one another. Those who once fought come to agreement.

All because its inhabitants recognized their Creator.

Lord, I praise You for the blessing You've poured out on my country. May we turn to You in praise every day.

October 14

"Give, and it shall be given unto you;
good measure, pressed down,
and shaken together, and running over,
shall men give into your bosom."
LUKE 6:38, KJV

You want me to what? Jake didn't say it, but he might as well have. His Sunday school teacher could see the thought on his face. As they continued discussing tithing, Jake didn't say much—his body language spoke for him. He crossed his arms and waited.

Finally Jake said, *"Ten percent?* I already give to God when I can afford it, and I do lots of things for the church. Isn't that enough?"

Stinginess with God really doesn't hurt Him. He already owns all creation. We only hurt ourselves when we try to bargain God down to 9 percent, 8 percent. . .and then point out our own good points to make up for our lack of giving.

God wants to give to a generous giver. But He can't give to you if you hold your cash tightly to your chest. How can you take, when your hands are full?

Are your hands wide open today?

Lord, help me to understand Your blessing of giving. I want to be generous and openhearted to You.

October 15

*Anyone who does not do what is right
is not a child of God; nor is
anyone who does not love his brother.*
1 JOHN 3:10

All of us have known a "nice person" we'd like to think will enter God's kingdom—someone like Rick, who'd give you the shirt off his back—but won't go to church, lives with his girlfriend, and can't get along with his parents. We love the world's Ricks and want them to share eternity with us, but when we mention God, they skitter away as if we'd burned them.

We can't exactly judge who knows Jesus and who doesn't. After all, we can't see into every heart. But lifestyle is a pretty good heart indicator: People who love God don't avoid Him or His commandments.

If there's a "Rick" in your life, pray for him. Ask God to unlock his heart, preparing the way for your witness. But if all you say falls on deaf ears, keep loving him—God may combine your loving care with someone else's words to win your friend.

Lord, help me reach out with loving-kindness and gentle words to the "Ricks" I see each day.

October 16

"Lord," Ananias answered,
*"I have heard many reports about this man
and all the harm he has done to your saints
in Jerusalem. And he has come here
with authority from the chief priests
to arrest all who call on your name."*
Acts 9:13–14

Ananias had just gotten a message from God. Could he have it right? *Visit the big-time Christian hunter, Saul?* That guy wasn't safe for Christians to be around.

Ananias wasn't stupid. He didn't want to spend the rest of his—possibly short—life in a nasty jail cell. *"Saul,* Lord? You want me to visit *him?"*

God understood Ananias's fears and didn't chide him for lack of faith. He explained this strange call.

God does speak to you. Sometimes it's through His Word—a verse you know you need to obey. Other times, His still, small voice tells your heart what to do or you go on a hunch. Like Ananias, at times you need to question a message. If so, do it in humble obedience, and God will let you know.

If He doesn't, you probably weren't hearing from Him after all.

Lord, help me discern Your call. If I miss one message, please repeat that call and ready my heart to answer it.

October 17

He who has the Son has life;
he who does not have
the Son of God does not have life.
1 JOHN 5:12

Many non-Christians would like to believe that religion is a smorgasbord affair: You can take a little here, a little there, and come up with your own brand. Take what you like, and leave the rest behind! All enter heaven, no matter their beliefs.

Such people have often belittled Christians for their "narrow" idea that there is only one truth—only those who believe in Jesus enter heaven. Even if you're a firm believer, you may feel uncomfortable defining a truth that leaves so many outside heaven's gates. But you aren't being ruled by your own thinking or a nasty desire to exclude anyone. If that *were* true, you'd keep the Good News to yourself.

Sure it's easier to keep your mouth shut. But then wouldn't you be trying to exclude others? It would be like holding the door to heaven shut.

Are you opening heaven's door today?

Jesus, I know it's not popular to tell others that You are the only way to heaven. Don't let that stop me from telling them the truth.

October 18

Who can find a virtuous women?
for her price is far above rubies.
PROVERBS 31:10, KJV

When you date someone, do you look for the best-looking girl around, the guy with the most money—or a person with good character?

Dreams of your future spouse probably include a great-looking person, romantic evenings together, and wonderful conversations. You may not imagine a man who's truthful or a woman who treats her parents with respect.

God doesn't say you can't marry a good-looking mate or even one with a hefty bank account. But you could live without them. You can't live happily with a weak character.

Character doesn't look glamorous. You can't show off by sending your friend a picture of it. But you can live with it for a happy lifetime. You'll never worry where your mate is when you know he's trustworthy. You'll never fear a family get-together when you know she'll treat your parents kindly.

Is your date a noble character—or just a character?

Lord, character may not be the asset I'm dreaming of, but I know it's important. Turn my heart toward someone with a strong love for You and the willingness to do right.

October 19

We instructed you how to live in order to please God, as in fact you are living. Now we ask you and urge you in the Lord Jesus to do this more and more.
1 THESSALONIANS 4:1

Alice had known Jesus for years, but her spiritual life didn't have the zip her best friend Darla's had.

"I'm afraid to witness to anyone," Alice admitted. "I might bore them to death. What do you have that I missed out on?"

Sometimes being a Christian can turn into drudgery. We know the truth; we're not committing any "major" sins; but our spiritual life seems to have stagnated. Where did we go wrong?

When knowing God has as much excitement as a drive through a desert, check to see you're following the instructions He already gave you. Are you spending time with Jesus through regular Bible reading and prayer? Have you confessed *all* sin? Are you spending time with Christians who uplift you?

Like Alice, all Christians have dry spells. Just don't let your life become a desert. Search for the water of God's Spirit and drink deeply at His well.

Jesus, I don't want to live in a desert when I can drink of Your Spirit. Fill me with Your love.

October 20

*Therefore confess your sins to each other
and pray for each other so that
you may be healed.
The prayer of a righteous man is
powerful and effective.*
JAMES 5:16

Kent hadn't seen Howard in months. They'd kind of lost touch. So when he heard that his friend had walked away from the Lord, he felt terrible.

"If I'd known, maybe I could have helped," Kent lamented to his mom. "If only I'd gotten his phone number when he moved!"

Kent had often thought of Howard and wondered how he was. *If only I'd prayed for him,* Kent thought.

If you have a friend you've lost touch with, you can still keep in touch. God has a marvelous way for you to keep on caring: prayer. Though you may not be able to call, write, or see each other, you still have a divine connection.

Lift your friend up to God in prayer, and the next time you see each other, it may be as if you were never apart. Prayer draws you close in ways talking never could.

Bring to mind those I need to pray for, Lord. May Your Spirit bring their needs to my heart.

October 21

*"Only in his hometown,
among his relatives and in his own house
is a prophet without honor."*
MARK 6:4

If you're the first in your family to know *Jesus,* instead of just religion, you may have days when you get in heated discussions, hear all kinds of accusations, and almost wish you'd never been the one God called.

Breaking new ground for Jesus is tough. All people—even non-Christians—hold their spiritual beliefs firmly and with strong emotion. Sometimes Satan has a strong hold on people, and they struggle when they hear the truth.

When your siblings aren't polite about their thoughts on your faith, your parents ignore your witness, or your cousin says, "It's just a stage you're going through," stand firm. Even Jesus didn't get *everyone* to listen to Him, and the Old Testament prophets got more abuse than you probably ever will.

The witness still goes on, and people come to Jesus every day. Maybe soon it will be that cousin who belittled you.

Lord, I need to trust in You, even when people don't listen to my words. Keep me firm in faith, and give me the words You'd have me share with them.

October 22

*"And he said, That which cometh out of the man,
that defileth the man. For from within,
out of the heart of men,
proceed evil thoughts."*
MARK 7:20–21, KJV

The devil tempted me, and I fell!" is no excuse for Christians. We can't get away with that line, any more than Adam got away with blaming Eve.

Though Satan is real and does tempt us, we can't evade our own responsibility. Jesus makes it clear that the real fault isn't in our environment, Satan, or anyone else. Our own sick hearts lead us into sin.

Jesus lived in the same pressure-cooker world we do, with sin all around Him, but He never gave in. Though religious leaders of His day erred, the Son of God stood firm in righteousness because His clean heart held no place for sin.

Left to ourselves, our case is hopeless—we can never change—but the Master is in the heart-cleaning business. Give Him yours today.

Lord, even when I want to be clean, my heart betrays me. Wash it clean in Your blood today.

October 23

*Their hearts are always going astray,
and they have not known my ways. . . .
They shall never enter my rest.*
HEBREWS 3:10–11

Cats always want to keep their options open. Close the door, and they'll try to open it again, even if they don't want to come into the room. They just want to be able to, if they change their minds later.

As a Christian, do you fear closing the door on other faiths or unscriptural ideas? Are you trying to leave your options open, or are you committed to Christ, having left behind old beliefs and ways?

Those who commit to Christ, then wander away, need to look at what they really believe. Sure, we all sin, but those who have really trusted Jesus don't constantly wobble in their faith—going first to this side and then to that.

God tested the Hebrews in the desert, and they wobbled big-time. Their actions showed what they believed in their hearts, and because their hearts had kept their options open, God said they'd never enter His eternal rest.

What is in your heart today?

Lord, I don't want to wobble. Draw me so close to You that I will never leave Your side.

October 24

*I praise you because I am fearfully
and wonderfully made;
your works are wonderful.*
PSALM 139:14

If all humanity worked for years on it, we'd never create a wonder like the human body. Imagine designing various body-part cells, each working smoothly and reproducing its very own sort. How much time would it take to make every atom of a healthy body work in sync with the others?

God created all this—and more—just out of His head. No laboratory, no special equipment; the Creator's mind alone worked it out in amazing detail, made it, and set this "invention" in an equally marvelous world.

When people try to tell you that everything in our universe "just happened," it's time to ask questions. Wouldn't it have taken a mighty intelligence, not just "accident" to plan all this?

But it's not just the universe—-*you* are wonderfully created, made to a special design, with your own fingerprints, face, and body chemistry. On top of that, God says you're wonderful.

Shouldn't something so wonderful serve Him?

Lord, I don't think of myself as wonderful most days. I praise You for taking such care over my design. Use me for Your kingdom's business.

October 25

*And who knows but that you have come
to royal position for such a time as this?*
ESTHER 4:14

Esther hadn't wanted to become the wife of a
pagan king and the queen of Persia. She got caught
in that situation and simply tried to make the best
of it.

The plots of Haman, the king's wicked advisor,
against her people, the Jews, thrust her into political
intrigue. When Esther's cousin, Mordecai, asked her
to intervene, she squirmed at the idea. Approaching
the king could mean her death. Could she risk it?

Mordecai reminded her that God was still in
control. Perhaps He had put her in this place to do
this act. So Esther did God's will.

We know how Esther felt. Sometimes we end
up in messy—even dangerous—situations we didn't
bring on ourselves. We wish we'd never gotten involved. Though we went in innocently, it backfired
on us.

In such a situation, maybe God has a purpose
for us. After all, He still controls our lives, too. All
we need to do is obey.

*Lord, when life gets messy, keep my eyes on You. I
need Your wisdom to make the right choices and to
do Your will.*

October 26

*I have not a cake, but an handful of meal
in a barrel, and a little oil in a cruse:
and, behold, I am gathering two sticks,
that I may go in and dress it for me and my son,
that we may eat it, and die.*
1 KINGS 17:12, KJV

The widow of Zarephath was desperate. In the middle of a drought, she had no food and no hope of getting any. She gave up. It was the end for both her and her son.

In that moment, Elijah entered her life, and a seemingly chance meeting set her back on track. She didn't have roast beef every day, just enough food for her and her family, but God took care of her.

Like the widow, despair knows your name. But no matter what the situation, it isn't time to give up! Even when life seems impossible, God still has hold of the possibilities. Some days, you may lose hope. It seems as if God has forgotten you, and the world is against you. But none of those thoughts come from God. He's told you He'll never fail you.

Help could be right around the corner!

Though I can't see the future, I know You can, Lord. Give me hope on those despair-filled days.

October 27

I hate double-minded men,
but I love your law.
PSALM 119:113

Have you ever run into a double-minded person? It can drive you nuts!

A double-minded person believes one thing—until another person tries to sway him. Then he changes his mind. If a friend is double-minded, you'll always wonder if he will meet you when he said he will, support the cause he said he would help with, or move somewhere else on the spur of the moment. You'll never know what's up!

Double-minded people don't have a guide they follow consistently. If public opinion changes, so do they. Disapproval from a family member may sway them—today.

That's no way to live. Everyone needs to have certain standards, codes of conduct, and personal rules.

God's laws give us the guidelines we need to avoid double-mindedness. When we know what's wrong, we won't do it, even if public opinion says it's right. If a friend doesn't agree with us, we'll know why we won't change our minds. We're single-minded.

Lord, I don't want to sway in the breeze on every issue. Keep me firm in Your Word so I know Your laws.

October 28

Shall I acquit a man with dishonest scales,
with a bag of false weights?
MICAH 6:11

God takes wrongdoing seriously—much more seriously than we're likely to do.

Sometimes we'd like to fudge a little. Maybe we take a box of pencils from work and excuse ourselves with the idea that we do work at home once in a while, and we'll need them. We think we don't harm anyone if we take that little extra. We slide it behind our backs, and an hour later it doesn't bother us.

But it bothers God just as much as it bothered Him that the merchants of Judah were shortchanging customers. They used lighter weights, which meant less product for the customers and more money for them.

God is so holy that He can't ignore wrongdoing. Mismeasuring their goods was just a sign of the evil that lived in the merchants' hearts. They were more caught up in their profit than their love for God.

Don't ask God to ignore your sin. He'd be disregarding the love that's missing in your heart.

Thank You, Lord, that You don't leave me in my sin, even when it only seems to weigh as much as a box of pencils.

October 29

He reveals deep and hidden things; he knows what lies in darkness, and light dwells with him.
DANIEL 2:22

Daniel and his friends, faced with the prospect of losing their lives, didn't run or sit up all night trying to find a solution. They prayed.

And to Daniel, God revealed Nebuchadnezzar's dream, complete with interpretation. It was as if the prophet were seeing into the king's mind.

Sometimes, like Daniel, you wish you knew what was in another person's head. You can't always know why a friend acted impulsively or what made your sibling act irrationally. People are complex.

But when you're in doubt about another's thinking, it's comforting to know that One knows exactly what's going on. God may never tell you all the details, but He can smooth your path when you have to confront a friend or try to make peace with a coworker. Pray, and though you may never know why, things can work out.

Lord, when people baffle me, I need Your wisdom. Reach into my relationships and bring understanding where we've created confusion. Touch my life with Your peace.

October 30

Blessed be the LORD God of our fathers,
which hath put such a thing as this
in the king's heart, to beautify the house
of the LORD which is in Jersalem.
EZRA 7:27, KJV

Sometimes government seems out of control. You vote because you've learned that good citizens do that, but you wonder if you have any impact. As elected officials take part in evil acts, you wonder, *Is it worth it?* But if everyone who knows God steps out of the political process, wickedness only increases.

God may call you to help out the campaign of a politician with strong morality. Or you could write letters to congressional members, telling them how they should vote on an issue.

Do something else every day, too—pray. God changes the course of politics. He did that for Ezra, when King Artaxerxes, a pagan king, opened the door so that Ezra could help rebuild Jerusalem.

He can rebuild our nation, too.

When politics seems out of control, Lord, help me to remember that everything in life is under Your control.

October 31

I looked for a man among them
who would build up the wall
and stand before me in the gap.
EZEKIEL 22:30

Martin Luther didn't want to gain the attention of all Europe; the humble university professor just had questions he wanted the church to discuss.

Luther was angry at the way the church had misled people. He wanted leaders to right the wrongs of tradition and greed and follow the teaching of Scripture. So on October 31, 1517, he posted ninety-five questions on the medieval equivalent of a bulletin board—the church door.

When people read his words, the furor started. His questions spread throughout his country, and many began to question what the church was doing. Wasn't what this monk said the truth?

God needed a man who would stand in the gap for Him, and Martin Luther did just that. Luther paid a high price: excommunication from the church, attacks from many scholars, and abuse from many who disagreed with him. But many people came to really know God through his teachings.

Is there a gap with your name on it today?

Jesus, when You need me to stand in the gap, give me strength to speak out for You.

November 1

*Like a gold ring in a pig's snout is
a beautiful woman who shows no discretion.*
PROVERBS 11:22

Remember, the Jewish people have never held the pig in very high esteem. They would not think of wasting valuable gold to adorn an animal they believed unclean. After all, all the gold in the world would never make a pig clean. You might as well throw the gold into the ocean.

In the same way, beauty is wasted on an immoral woman. She may look good with her golden adornments and beautiful face, but a pig is a pig is a pig.

Does this sound harsh and unforgiving? Can't people change and reform? Of course they can. Unlike a pig, a person can be cleansed of sins through confession, forgiveness, and reformation. We all sin in various ways, and it's not for us to judge too harshly or refuse to recognize real change in a person.

But it is our job to use discretion in choosing our companions. Know who you are dating, keep your standards high, and don't be fooled by outward appearances.

Father, help me maintain my standards while avoiding judgment on the worth of others. It's a hard line to walk, but I know You will help me.

November 2

*Speak up for those who
cannot speak for themselves,
for the rights of all who are destitute.
Speak up and judge fairly;
defend the rights of the poor and needy.*
PROVERBS 31:8–9

Jesus made it quite clear that every one of us is responsible for defending the rights of the poor and needy, but what does that mean in our everyday life? How can one person make that much difference?

We each have a vote and the responsibility to use it wisely. Where do the candidates in this election stand on human rights? What laws are they promising to make, and how will they effect the poor? What have they done in the past that foretells what they will do in the future? You don't have to make a big study of this—you'll get the drift easily enough.

There's plenty of room for differing opinions in this country, and no one should vote on the basis of only one issue, but how an election will affect the lives of the poor should be kept in mind. Compassion is never so simple as merely Republican versus Democrat.

Father, when I vote, help me do so wisely, keeping the fate of the poor and needy in mind, no matter what my party preference may be.

November 3

I know how to live on almost nothing or with everything. I have learned the secret of living in every situation, whether it is with a full stomach or empty, with plenty or little.
PHILIPPIANS 4:12, NLT

No one knows what the future will bring. Some struggle their whole lives with no visible signs of success for their efforts, while others zoom to the top and stay there. Most of us bounce around a lot, finding success in some things and failure in others.

Some people literally wish their lives away. "In six months, I'll get a raise," they say, blowing off the days between now and then as if they were unimportant. Why not have a good time in the present instead of wasting those six months? The raise may or may not come, but today is here for the taking and will never come again.

Father, teach me not to waste any of my life while I wait for things to get better, to take each day as it comes and enjoy it to the fullest.

November 4

Woe to him who quarrels with his Maker.
ISAIAH 45:9

It's a good thing this verse doesn't say, "Woe to him who complains to his Maker," or we'd all be in trouble. As it is, we often skate on pretty thin ice, because quarreling, complaining, and moaning and groaning are all a little too close for comfort.

Why doesn't God "fix" the things that are wrong in our lives?

The Bible tells us we're just the clay He works with, and how often does a pot complain to the potter? "I'd like to be a little thinner, if you don't mind." It's a stupid idea, because the potter makes what he needs, and the clay has no voice in the creation. What's the clay know about the potter's needs and plans?

In the end, we and everything else in the world are whatever God wants us to be, and arguing about it is a waste of time and energy. Be the best pot you can be, and leave the rest to the Potter.

Father, I trust Your plans for me and my world. I don't know enough to argue about it, and it's not my place to do so. Forgive me when I become impatient.

November 5

His commands are not burdensome,
for everyone born of God
overcomes the world.
1 JOHN 5:3–4

Suppose your doctor told you, "I can guarantee that you will live for two hundred years if you do exactly what I tell you," and then gave you a list of directions. In addition, he would give you the phone numbers of twenty people living according to his directions—all of them happily healthy and remarkably old—and these people would teach you how to follow the directions and give you all the help they could.

You'd try it, wouldn't you? But a couple of the directions would be difficult for you, even with help, and sometimes you would fail. The next time you saw the doctor, you'd confess that you had failed, expecting the worst, but the doctor would say, "That's okay. Do you still believe in me?" You'd say yes and he'd say, "I forgive you. Start over."

Would you consider the doctor's directions a burden or a blessing? How does this make you feel about God's commandments and His promise of eternal life?

Father, thank You for showing me how to live and inherit eternal life through obeying Your commands, which are not a burden, but a blessing to me.

November 6

So I commend the enjoyment of life,
because nothing is better for a man
under the sun than to
eat and drink and be glad.
ECCLESIASTES 8:15

You don't have to be a sourpuss to be a good Christian. There are rules and regulations that need to be attended to, but they are not meant to take the joy out of life. Just the opposite: They are meant to make life better for everyone.

Sometimes we take ourselves far too seriously, as if enjoying ourselves were a sign of weakness or a sin that would bar us from heaven. Sure, there are things forbidden to us, but much more is allowed. We don't have to drag ourselves miserably through this life in hopes of enjoying the next. What a waste that would be, what disrespect for the One who created us and our world and proclaimed them good. How can you rejoice in God and praise His Name while refusing to enjoy the gifts He has given you?

Father, thank You for all the bright and wonderful gifts You have given me. May I enjoy them with my whole heart so others will see the wonder of Your love.

November 7

*Everyone who competes in the games
goes into strict training. They do it
to get a crown that will not last;
but we do it to get a crown
that will last forever.*
1 CORINTHIANS 9:25

Do you work out to keep your body in decent shape? It takes a lot of determination and effort, but you keep at it because you know it will result in a longer, healthier life. Of course, in time your body will still fail, no matter how hard you train. There's no way around that, but you do everything you can to put it off a little longer.

What about your spiritual training? Do you give an equal amount of time and energy to that? Do you study the Bible, your spiritual training manual, and obey its commands? Do you take advantage of the personal trainers who are willing to help you at no charge? When you get in spiritual shape, do you help others with their training?

Physical training can only take you so far. Spiritual training is for eternity.

Lord, don't let me ignore the fitness of my soul, which is far more important in the long run than the fitness of my body.

November 8

And be not conformed to this world:
but be ye transformed by
the renewing of your mind.
ROMANS 12:2, KJV

The world is full of amateur tailors trying to make us fit into their patterns, even if they have to squeeze and push us into them. If we don't fit, they will claim it's not because their pattern is wrong—something's wrong with us.

Some friends think a weekend without getting drunk is a waste of time. If they can't convince you to come along, they'll find someone else to spend time with, because you obviously don't fit in.

If you've got your mind straight, this won't bother you. You wouldn't wear a pair of jeans that came up to your knees, so why should you try to be something you aren't? You're not stamped out of a mold—you're an individual with your own mind. Don't let anyone convince you that you need to conform to their pattern.

Father, thank You for helping me set my own priorities. Give me the strength to resist those who want me to ignore my values and adopt their own.

November 9

The LORD your God is with you,
he is mighty to save.
He will take great delight in you,
he will quiet you with his love,
he will rejoice over you with singing.
ZEPHANIAH 3:17

What's your first reaction to this verse?

"Who, me?" It's a little mind-boggling, isn't it? The Lord wants to save you from your enemies, just as He did for David. He takes delight in you—you make Him smile. When you're upset, His love will calm you. And when you come to Him, He will sing a song of joy.

The Bible's not talking about a group of people, either. It's talking about *you,* with all your fears and all your faults. With all the billions of people in this world, all the stars in the sky, all the other forms of life here or elsewhere, God is not too busy for you. When you fall in love, God is happy with you. When you have a child, He rejoices with you. When you suffer, He suffers. When you laugh, He laughs.

How do you repay love like that? The only way you can—with love.

Father, thank You for Your unbounded love. I know I am unworthy, but I am so grateful You care so much for me.

November 10

Who would complain if they suddenly found themselves rich or were promoted to positions of responsibility? Not too many of us. Everyone loves the idea of a windfall, but the truth is, your work has just begun when you see your dreams fulfilled.

When you have nothing, no one expects very much from you. Someone who stocks shelves is not expected to worry about the quality of the merchandise or the foreign exchange rate, but if a shelf stocker is suddenly put in charge of purchasing, he has to scramble to learn everything that goes with the new job and handle his new responsibilities.

None of that is bad or to be avoided, as long as you realize there's no such thing as a free lunch. Success comes from hard work and leads to even harder work.

Father, help me remember that it'll be a long time before I can rest on my laurels in this world. The more I have, the more will be required of me.

November 11

For I am persuaded, that neither death, nor life,
nor angels, nor principalities, nor powers,
nor things present, nor things to come,
nor height, nor depth, nor any other creature,
shall be able to separate us from the love of God,
which is in Christ Jesus our Lord.
ROMANS 8:38–39, KJV

A lot of things try to separate us from God. We trip on our own sins or over the feet of those we're walking with. We get "too busy" to attend church or too "educated" to trust the Bible. We often forget about God's love in our daily lives, turning to it only when we find ourselves in trouble. Our memory is pretty short, and God seems far away.

Yet none of this or "anything else in all creation" (NIV) makes God give up on us. His love is always there for us, in good times or bad, success or failure, sin or sanctity. We can always go home to Him, no matter how far we stray.

You may have given up on yourself, but God hasn't. Accept His constant love and forgiveness, no matter how undeserving you feel.

Father, I often feel unworthy of anyone's love, especially Yours. In times like that, remind me that You will never give up on me.

November 12

*A good name is more desirable
than great riches;
to be esteemed is better
than silver or gold.*
PROVERBS 22:1

Life offers us a lot of opportunities to cheat and get away with it. Creative cheaters can bluff their way into amazing salaries, high public office, or tax refunds large enough to support a small nation, and they seem to get away with it most of the time.

When they do, it's not always because they're so clever that no one notices. Sometimes, the people around them are perfectly aware of the cheating going on—but for reasons of their own, they look the other way. But they usually know who's a cheat, and they would never trust those people with much of value.

The next time you're tempted to cheat a little, ask yourself if it's worth the consequences. What would you prefer to see on your tombstone? "Here lies an honest man" or "He was successful, but . . ."?

Father, there are many ways to get to the top. Help me choose the ones that earn me the respect of others, even if the path is a little longer and harder.

November 13

Be strong and courageous.
Do not be terrified;
do not be discouraged,
for the LORD your God will be with you
wherever you go.
JOSHUA 1:9

We all spend a lot of time being terrified. And it's true, there's plenty out there to scare us, but not nearly as much as the news reports or movies would seem to indicate.

You can't let yourself be paralyzed by fear or become a prisoner of terror. You need to take some precautions, but you have a life to lead. In times like these, it helps to remember that God is always with you, urging you to be strong and courageous. Find a balance between caution and trust that will allow you to live a full, satisfying, and reasonably safe life.

Father, thank You for Your comfort and protection, which give me the confidence I need to lead a full life in a world that is never perfectly safe.

November 14

You can talk to a psychic today through an 800 number instead of having to travel to the top of a faraway mountain. Isn't progress wonderful? Instant sin! For free.

The world has always had people willing to tell fortunes, give advice, or put the gullible in touch with their past lives. Some of them seem to give sensible advice, and if you read their books, they can give you a good feeling about yourself—something that's hard to find in the real world—but that's about all.

Some of these people claim to be prophets speaking for God. How can you deal with that? Well, the truth is, there hasn't been much work for prophets since Christ came on the scene, so skepticism is always in order.

If you need a peek into your future, why not go to the source? Ask God. Sometimes you will get an answer, sometimes you won't, but at least you can trust those answers you get. Don't dirty yourself with spiritualism that is not based on the Lord your God.

Father, teach me to seek my answers from You, not from anyone else.

November 15

Remember ye not the former things,
neither consider the things of old.
ISAIAH 43:18, KJV

The study of history is always profitable, as long as we don't get stuck in the past. "We've always done it this way" does not guarantee that we've always done it right. We need to respect the wisdom of experience without making a little god of it.

Dwelling on the past can stop you dead in your tracks. Suppose you went into a big meeting and made a total fool of yourself. Does that mean you should avoid all future meetings? Not if you learned from the experience and don't make the same mistake at every meeting. If you don't go to the meetings, you don't get ahead, so take the chance. Don't dwell on the past.

Life's full of embarrassing moments we'd prefer to forget, and people will usually allow us to put these moments behind us. After all, they have had their own share of such moments, and some of them have been bigger bloopers than any of yours.

Father, help me get past my mistakes and get on with my future, knowing You will help me guard my mouth and cover my back when needed.

November 16

Do not cut your bodies for the dead
or put tattoo marks on yourselves.
I am the LORD.
LEVITICUS 19:28

Tattoos are in, not to mention body piercing and other forms of personal mutilation. Some see them as personal statements: "It's my body, and I'll do what I like with it."

Sorry, folks, but it's *not* your body. "Do not offer the parts of your body to sin, as instruments of wickedness, but rather offer yourselves to God, as those who have been brought from death to life; and offer the parts of your body to him as instruments of righteousness" (Romans 6:13).

When you ask God to take care of your soul, your body is part of the deal. You are all His, and He does not want mutilated sacrifices. Your body is God's temple. He lives in you and through you, and you should no more desecrate that temple than you should take an ax to an altar.

Father, fads and fashions should never make me present a less-than-perfect sacrifice to You. Give me the strength I need to avoid anything that lessens my dedication to You.

November 17

Parents apparently haven't changed all that much in the last 2,000 years. Neither have children. As much as children and parents love each other, they manage to drive each other crazy.

As you grow older, you will begin to find yourself resembling your father or your mother (or maybe both of them!). You won't like it at first, but in time you will be able to see past the annoying things and realize that they always had your best interests at heart. However they managed to show it, your mother and father loved you, and they always will—just as you love them. When the time comes for you to be a parent, remember how you used to feel and try to do as good a job as they did.

Father, thank You for my parents. We don't always agree, but I'm coming to respect them more and more as I mature, and I know how hard I was on them at times.

November 18

*I broke the bars of your yoke
and enabled you to walk
with heads held high.*
LEVITICUS 26:13

God always wants us to walk with our heads held high, free and proud to be His children. A child of God will never be totally enslaved. The body may be captured, but inside the heart is total freedom.

Sometimes we look at people living without freedom and wonder why they put up with it. Why don't they fight back? Why don't they value themselves enough to chance a rebellion? We've been free for so long that we think "Give me liberty or give me death" is a universal sentiment.

But we don't know what's going on in the mind of another person. "Give me liberty or give me death" is a wonderful-sounding phrase, but how often have we had to back it up with the lives of our loved ones and ourselves? Others, faced with a struggle just to feed their children, may consider the phrase ridiculous. If their children survive, that's freedom enough, and they can still walk with their heads held high.

Father, thank You for allowing me to live in a country where freedom is valued and protected. As Your child, I will always be free in my heart, no matter what the circumstances.

November 19

*Encourage the young men to
be self-controlled.*
TITUS 2:6

Ever since potty training, you've been learning self-control, and by now you're pretty sick of it. You have to control yourself on dates, at work, while driving or eating. Even your thoughts need to be controlled most of the time. Does it ever end?

Nope. But it does change. You get older, and self-control is easier. Not so many rampaging hormones, for one thing. You develop more consideration for others and tend to fly off the handle less frequently. Eventually you find the perfect balance point between your desires and civilization's expectations, and it's at that point that you become truly productive and fulfilled.

You can control yourself or let society control you, and society is a lot rougher on you. A lack of self-control will cost you jobs, love, and even jail time. When looked at logically, learning self-control is the easy way out.

Father, give me self-control when I need it and teach me how to develop it on my own so I can be a productive member of society and not endanger others to satisfy myself.

November 20

*Rejoice not when thine enemy falleth, and
let not thine heart be glad when he stumbleth:
Lest the L{\scriptsize ORD} see it, and it displease him,
and he turn away his wrath from him.*
P{\scriptsize ROVERBS} 24:17–18, KJV

Here's an interesting angle on why we shouldn't clap when our enemies suffer. Our natural tendency is to be happy when the bully finally hits the playground dirt or the dictator disappears some dark night. He's gotten away with it for too long, and we rejoice when he gets his due.

But God knows the bully and the dictator. One day His wrath will fall on them, without any help from us. He also doesn't want any cheering from the sidelines, any self-righteous gloating, any songs of joy—even ones that are hidden in our hearts. If He hears them, He will disapprove of them and turn away His wrath before the job is done. God respects everyone, good or bad, and expects us to do the same. We may not always be able to love our enemies the way God commands, but we don't have to show joy at anyone's downfall.

Father, sometimes it's hard to respect those who don't respect me, but justice is Your job, not ours. Teach me how to love my enemies as You command.

November 21

There was a man all alone;
he had neither son nor brother.
There was no end to his toil,
yet his eyes were not content
with his wealth. "For whom
am I toiling," he asked,
"and why am I depriving
myself of enjoyment?"
ECCLESIASTES 4:8

This fellow had to work his land alone, with no help from his family. He apparently did a good job of it, but he wasn't satisfied with the wealth his hard work provided. What more could he possibly do? He certainly couldn't work harder or longer, but unless he did, he wouldn't get any richer.

Finally he realized his priorities were out of order. He had more than enough for himself and no one to carry on after him. If he had someone to inherit his wealth, that would be one thing, but he didn't, so why shouldn't he take a little time for fun?

It's easy to get caught up in the race to accumulate—but if you think like this long enough, life becomes a drag. No fun, all work, week after week. Every once in a while, take a hard look at your priorities.

Father, help me be content with my wealth, such as it is, and know when it's time for a little rest and relaxation.

November 22

Let your gentleness be evident to all.
PHILIPPIANS 4:5

Gentleness doesn't seem to have much going for it today. It's macho time, every man for himself, and heaven help the weak. At least that's what the movies and television tell us, and a lot of people seem to be buying into it.

But movies and television aren't into reporting the truth. They're into entertaining, and gentleness can look boring, even in 3-D. For every graphic murder scene in the news, there are at least 1,000 acts of kindness that go unreported. For every man who strikes out in anger, there are 1,000 who reach out in peace. For every maniac oppressor, there are 1,000 Peace Corps volunteers.

Once in a while, you'll see a story about a good person—usually around Christmas—but John Wayne and Jimmy Stewart are dead. Who are our role models today? For the good of the world, "Let your gentleness be evident to all."

Father, teach me how to be that rare and endangered species—a gentle man, one who gives of himself for the benefit of others.

November 23

Examine yourselves, whether ye be in the faith;
prove your own selves.
2 CORINTHIANS 13:5, KJV

Oh, no, not another test! And it's not even going to be multiple choice.

Still, a little introspection is always a good idea. At least you'll know how far off the mark you've wandered. So what are the criteria here? Who gets an A and who fails?

First of all, this is an open-book test. Take your Bible and read all of Matthew. Read every word Jesus spoke and every command He ever gave. Point by point, how did you come out? Give yourself a grade on every command.

It could be kind of dismal until you hit Matthew 22:37–39: " 'Love the Lord your God with all your heart and with all your soul and with all your mind.' This is the first and greatest commandment. And the second is like it: 'Love your neighbor as yourself.'"

Now throw away your entire test. This is the only question that counts. By the way, the person doing the grading is you, and you can grade on a curve. Not so hard, was it?

Father, in a real test, I'm sure I'd fail, but You forgive me and only require my love. I can do that.

November 24

Remember this:
Whoever sows sparingly
will also reap sparingly,
and whoever sows generously
will also reap generously.
2 CORINTHIANS 9:6

If you want a good crop, you can't toss one seed out every few feet and hope nature will fill in the spaces between them. Seed costs money, but you have to invest in it before you have anything to harvest.

The same principle holds true for other things in life. If you want love, you have to let yourself be vulnerable. Sometimes the crop will fail, but if you can't invest yourself emotionally, you never have a chance of finding love. If you want success in your work, you will need to invest time and effort before you see the first shoots of success. If you want a happy family, you have to be there for your spouse and children.

Sometimes these investments are hard to make. You have little time, effort, or money to spare and may want to hang onto what you have, not risking it on less than a sure shot. But few things in life are guaranteed. Invest now, while you are still young; one day you will reap generously.

Father, show me the investments I need to make now.

November 25

Give thanks to the LORD, call on his name;
make known among the nations
what he has done. Sing to him,
sing praise to him; tell of all
his wonderful acts.
1 CHRONICLES 16:8–9

We often think of giving thanks as a private event, something strictly between us and God. At most, we join together with our family or church in thanksgiving. Public thanksgiving makes us uneasy. We don't want to seem like we're boasting.

Yet the Bible urges us to sing His praises loudly for others to hear. But how do you do it?

Start small. The next time you feel you have been blessed, tell another believer. He'll tell someone else, and the story will get around, as all stories do. Once you feel comfortable talking about such things to believers, tell a close friend who isn't a churchgoer, speaking humbly but surely and then going on to another topic. In time you will find your comfort level. Good news is meant to be shared.

Father, give me the courage I need to sing Your praises and the discernment to know who needs to hear Your message.

November 26

Whatever you do, work at it with all your heart,
as working for the Lord, not for men,
since you know that you will receive
an inheritance from the Lord as a reward.
It is the Lord Christ you are serving.
COLOSSIANS 3:23–24

Are you miserable in your job? Mentally switch employers—imagine you work for God, not your boss.

Once you decide to work as if God were your boss, everything changes. You can't call in sick every Monday when God knows every healthy cell in your body. You can't give less than your best to God, who knows exactly how capable you are and wants to reward your efforts. If it takes fifty hours a week to get the job done, would you complain to God?

A few months of this, and your human supervisor is going to notice the change. You're getting the job done without resentment. Maybe you can be trusted, even promoted. She won't have the vaguest idea of what's come over you, but she'll be pleased, and supervisors who are pleased often turn into decent people. Try it.

Father, help me do all my work as if I were work-ing for You, no matter how bad conditions are for me.

November 27

We humans have a unique way of looking at the world: If we can't see it, it doesn't exist. Some really had a hard time believing the earth was round until they saw that little blue marble in pictures sent down from space. Others have no idea of how *big* a moose is until one is standing in the middle of the road, towering over their puny car. On television, they look a lot smaller.

But the earth has always been round, and the moose has always been big. Whether we've believed that or not, it's always been true.

Some people do not have faith for the same reason. They've never seen anything that proved God's faithfulness, so it doesn't exist for them. Does their disbelief make God's faithfulness disappear? If you say a moose is a big cow, isn't it still a moose? Things are what they are, no matter what we don't believe, and God is, and always has been, faithful to those who follow Him.

Father, You are who You are, unchangeable and forever. I may not be able to prove this, but I know it's true.

November 28

Finish your outdoor work
and get your fields ready;
after that, build your house.
PROVERBS 24:27

This verse speaks of a basic survival situation most of us never have to face, but it has a modern parallel. Money is scarce when you're young. The little extra you have can be invested in a decent apartment or a course that will help you in your work. Isn't it better to take the course and live in a shoebox apartment for a year? A new apartment won't give you any return on your investment, but new skills will have immediate results, securing your livelihood.

Life is full of hard choices, and waiting for future rewards is not easy, but a little effort in the right places can make all the difference in the world.

Father, help me make the right choices in where I invest my money and my work, even if it means I have to give up some things I want very much.

November 29

Who can discern his errors?
Forgive my hidden faults.
PSALM 19:12

The truth is, we all have lots of hidden faults that need confessing. Some we hide from others on purpose; some we even manage to hide from ourselves.

But God's grace is not limited by our limitations. He can see into the subconscious corners of our lives, and He can bring healing and cleansing to even those hidden dirty spots. When we can say "forgive my hidden faults" and really mean it, opening ourselves to God in complete trust and surrender, then He will change us in ways we never knew we needed.

Christ offers us total forgiveness from the secret sins we hide from others, afraid they wouldn't love us if they knew what we were really like—and He also forgives the deepest sin we hide even from ourselves.

Father, my sins are more numerous than I'll ever know, but I know Your forgiveness is complete.

November 30

I waited patiently for the LORD;
he turned to me and heard my cry.
He lifted me out of the slimy pit,
out of the mud and mire;
he set my feet on a rock and gave me
a firm place to stand.
PSALM 40:1–2

To continue the thought, God is your permanent four-wheel drive. You get bogged down up to your axles and He's there with the winch and the Jeep. As with most road services, you may have to wait patiently for Him to turn around and hear your cry, but He will get there, and He will always put you back on the road, no matter how deep a pit you've dug for yourself.

Of course it would have been better if you hadn't tried to drive where you had no business driving in the first place, but God is patient. He believes you will one day learn your lesson and stay on the road. Until then, He operates a twenty-four-hour rescue service for your benefit—at no charge.

Father, thank You for rescuing me time after time. Help me eventually learn my lesson and stay on the right road. Even when I don't, though, I know I can always count on You to save me.

December 1

Let us lay aside. . .sin
which doth so easily beset us. . .
Looking unto Jesus. . .who for the joy
that was set before him endured the cross.
HEBREWS 12:1–2, KJV

Y ou were enjoying a sport, not even thinking about your body, but getting into the game, when suddenly you moved the wrong way or someone hit you, and down you went. In a flash, you moved from pleasure to pain. The doctor diagnosed a sprained ankle—and you can't play sports for a while.

Temptation sidelines you just like a sports injury. You're going along, minding your own business, and suddenly it hits. In one moment a new spiritual weakness entangles you. Cleaning out that sin may not happen overnight. You may have to turn to God many days—and many times in a day—until it no longer tempts you.

But don't give up when sin attacks. Just like that sports injury, if you do the right things, it will heal. Bring it to Dr. Jesus, and someday that temptation won't even draw you.

Lord, keep me from sin. But when I do fall, help me not to avoid the cross You've set before me.

December 2

*Live a life of love,
just as Christ loved us
and gave himself up for us
as a fragrant offering
and sacrifice to God.*
EPHESIANS 5:2

Have you ever stored a Bible in a musty cellar? If you have, you know that the next time you use it had better *not* be in Bible study. No one will want to sit anywhere near you.

But the worst thing you could do isn't pulling out your smelly Bible—it's never pulling out your Bible at all.

Longtime Christians who never read the Word smell, too. They may look good when they whip out the pew Bible, but a few seconds later, when they can't find the passage, a rank odor wafts up. These Christians who dress up their coffee tables with their Bibles but never open them won't love others the way Jesus does, either. Their command of Scripture stinks.

Even using a stinky Bible every day helps you become more like the Master. Because the more you live in His love, the more you can smell like Jesus, who gave himself as a "fragrant offering" to God the Father.

Jesus, I don't want to be a stinky Christian. Keep me in Your Word every day.

December 3

*Commit to the LORD whatever you do,
and your plans will succeed.*
PROVERBS 16:3

W endy, your life is planned out to the final minute," Anne said with a little envy. "No one else knows just what they're doing three weeks from today at 2:00."

Wendy liked to organize her life. Her large planning notebook outlined her schedule for the next month—dental appointments, dates, even birthdays of distant cousins. She'd also set down her future. In the back of her book she'd even listed specific career goals and dates to achieve them.

A few short years later, Wendy discovered that her career wasn't on schedule. Nowhere *near* on schedule! Suddenly life seemed to be one big disappointment.

When she confided her "failure" to Anne, her best friend pointed out some facts. "You may not have the fastest-growing career in the world, but people appreciate everything you do for them. You're well paid for your work, and you like what you do. You've had lots of chances to tell people about Christ, too. What's your beef?"

That night, during her prayer time, Wendy knew her life was running according to plan. But the plan was God's, not hers.

Lord, show me Your purpose for my life. I want my plans to be Your plans.

December 4

So God created man in his own image,
in the image of God he created him;
male and female he created them.
God blessed them.
GENESIS 1:27–28

*Y*ou were created in God's image. God made you in a special design and blessed you.

But that special creation and blessing aren't yours alone. He also created and blessed the person you'll marry. Are you ready to treat your spouse as a person God has blessed? Do you remember that in His eyes you're *both* important? Can you keep each other from sin and encourage each other in your faith?

When you marry someone you know is created in God's image and realize just what that means, you don't mistreat your spouse. Though you may disappoint each other sometimes, you remember that this God-created person is special—not perfect. Sin may mar God's creation, but it cannot change the value of His work.

A believing man and wife are blessed by God. Even the most challenging life situations can't change that promise.

Jesus, I want to treat my spouse like a treasure from You. Help me see when I'm ready for the blessing of marriage.

December 5

For of this you can be sure:
No immoral, impure or greedy person—
such a man is an idolater—
has any inheritance in the kingdom
of Christ and of God.
EPHESIANS 5:5

No, Virginia, there isn't a Santa Claus.

But there was Saint Nicholas, a fourth-century bishop of Myra. According to legend, this generous man gave three poor girls gold for their dowry.

Nicholas became a popular saint in Holland, where he was called "Sinterklaas." When Dutch settlers came to America, they brought along their tradition that the generous saint gave children gifts on the eve of Saint Nicholas, December 5.

The Dutch custom influenced Clement Moore, who created Santa Claus, the jolly, red-suited, gift-giving fellow we recognize, in his poem " 'Twas the Night Before Christmas."

Saint Nicholas doesn't have much to do with Santa Claus—just as the original meaning of Christmas has nothing to do with holiday overspending and greed.

What are you looking forward to this Christmas? Fancy gifts or the birth of the Savior?

Lord, I don't want to give in to greed this season. Teach me instead to be a generous giver.

December 6

Buy the truth, and sell it not.
PROVERBS 23:23, KJV

If you tell my mother what happened, we're through," Rod stated emphatically.

Katie gave in to Rod's wishes, even though she thought he was being foolish. It wasn't that Rod had done anything wrong—until he lied to his mother and told her that the black eye came from a fall while skiing. Only Katie knew he'd actually been attacked by a couple of campus rowdies.

The lie burned into Katie's soul, though it didn't bother Rod at all.

Later Katie told the story to a friend. "I guess I should have known then that he wasn't a Christian, and I should have stopped dating him. But he talked like a Christian and seemed sincere in his faith. I never knew he was lying to me, either—just like he's lied to his mother. Stupid lies about unimportant things. Its like a sickness with him."

Katie had learned the hard way that Rod was not the "someone special" God had in mind for her. She stood up for her faith, and in time God brought along that special man for her.

Lord, I want to date the person You have in mind for me. I need Your wisdom to make the right decision, though.

December 7

Pride only breeds quarrels,
but wisdom is found in those
who take advice.
PROVERBS 13:10

Mr. Milton drives me crazy," Lisa admitted to a coworker. "Every other day he's criticizing my work. I almost snapped back at him."

Criticism isn't easy to take. At first, your mind wants to snap back with explanations and counter-criticisms. *Well, if I'd had enough time. . .If I'd gotten the right information. . .*

Maybe your objections are true, but giving a sharp answer won't help others appreciate your efforts. Pride can get in the way of good work.

When you are criticized, take a good look at the critique. *Were* you sloppy? *Could* you have done better? What would have helped you improve? Don't start with excuses, but look at it from your boss's point of view. Would you like your work if *you* were the boss?

If you've made mistakes, learn from them. Turn the critique into advice that helps you do better.

I know I'm not perfect, God, but sometimes it's hard to admit it to my boss. Keep our communication clear so pride can't lead us into quarrels.

December 8

He also told them this parable:
"Can a blind man lead a blind man?
Will they not both fall into a pit?"
LUKE 6:39

What a delightful description Jesus gave us in this parable. You can easily see this pair ending in a pit because neither can see the road.

Sometimes we're no better than these foolish men. Without even thinking of it, we hang on to someone who's going in the wrong direction. By the time we realize we've been following others, not God, we're on the edge of a crater.

Want to know if you will end in a spiritual hole? Look at the people you follow. Are they filled with peace and serving God, or are they running their own show, constantly dissatisfied with life?

Since you'll end up much like the people you follow most, be sure the people you emulate are worth following. Do they do what the Bible says is right? Are they honest and loving?

In the end, make sure you're following the greatest leader—Jesus. His paths don't go into pits.

Lord, I want to be a leader who won't bring others into a pit. Guide me this day to walk in Your footsteps.

December 9

*There came wise men from the east to Jerusalem,
saying, "Where is he that is born King of
the Jews? for we have seen his star in the east,
and are come to worship him."*
MATTHEW 2:1–2, KJV

Who are the magi? Tradition names them, numbers them, and describes their entourage, but the Bible's story is spare.

Suddenly, in the biblical account, the mysterious magi appear from the east, stop on Herod's doorstep, and ask for the king of the Jews. They don't explain where they came from. We don't know why only *they* saw the star. Or why others didn't come from the south and north—and even across the sea, from the west.

We can be certain these men didn't come from around the corner—or East Jerusalem. To get to their destination, they had to follow a star, not a road map. Weeks before the birth of the child, they were probably already on their way. Through the star, God called them. They put out a lot of effort for a God they barely knew.

Yet some of us have trouble driving around the corner to church!

Thank You, Jesus, that You called me to Yourself as You did the wise men. I want to be ready to travel the distance.

December 10

*In vain you rise early and stay up late,
toiling for food to eat—
for he grants sleep to those he loves.*
PSALM 127:2

If this is your employer's busy season, you drive into work when it's dark and don't get home until the stars are twinkling overhead. Even if you don't have to work overtime, you cram two hours' work into sixty minutes.

Wiped out by the time you get home, you grab a quick dinner, turn down your pastor's request for help on a Christmas project, write out a few Christmas cards, and drag yourself into bed. The next tired morning you start all over again.

Giving your all to pay the bills isn't life as God designed it. The Architect of our lives sees the bigger picture, and a job is only part of it. His blueprint for our lives has better things, and if he's building a castle, we don't want to settle for a cottage.

When we're so tired that God's blueprints start to look fuzzy to us, we need to meet with the Architect. Prayer and rest have a wonderful way of restoring us and bringing our lives into focus.

When work just overwhelms me, I need to get the plan back in focus, Lord. Turn my heart to You.

December 11

The Israelites ate manna for forty years. . .
until they reached the border of Canaan.
Exodus 16:35

You might call it "doing laps." Just as a swimmer goes back and forth in the pool to build up strength, sometimes God keeps us in the same place, doing the same thing, for a long time.

The Israelites complained that they didn't have food, so God gave them manna. . .today and tomorrow and the next day. Boy, were they sick of that white, waferlike stuff! Like the swimmer in the pool, they never got anything different.

In our spiritual walk, when we get stuck "doing laps," we need to take a look at ourselves. Maybe, like the Israelites, we've sinned, and God is trying to humble us. Or maybe we need to gain strength, so God has us exercising the same spiritual muscle over and over again.

If you're doing laps, search your heart. Do you need to confess some sin so you can move on? If not, don't get discouraged. God is building up your strength.

That's why you're diving into the water one more time.

Lord, when I feel waterlogged, show me why I'm diving into the water again.

December 12

*I press on to take hold of that for
which Christ Jesus took hold of me.*
PHILIPPIANS 3:12

Anyone who's been married for even a few months has probably run into the "favorite comfy clothes" problem. One spouse has a disreputable T-shirt, sweatshirt, or sweatpants. When the other tries to throw it out or add it to the rag pile, the owner objects. "That's my favorite T-shirt. I've had it since high school. Sure, I know the arm is almost ripped off, but I like it!"

Holding on to comfortable clothes, even if they aren't fashionable, won't hurt you much, as long as you and your spouse don't argue about it. But carry the same attitude over to your spiritual life, and you'll run into a lot of trouble.

A spiritual walk isn't made to be "comfy." God designed it to challenge you to grow. So don't pull on sin the way you'd put on your comfiest sweatshirt. God calls you to attack sin in your life, to fulfill His commands, and reach out to others.

Fight back against sin—and press on!

Father, don't let me get comfortable in sin. Challenge me to clothe myself in a holy robe, not a holey T-shirt.

December 13

As ye have always obeyed,
not as in my presence only,
but now much more in my absence,
work out your own salvation
with fear and trembling.
PHILIPPIANS 2:12, KJV

Now that you are on your own, it's easy to think, *Mom and Dad aren't here to yell at me. I'll just do things my way.* Well, when it comes to how you vacuum your apartment, it doesn't matter if you don't obey Mom and Dad's rules, as long as things get clean. But moral choices *do* matter.

Mom and Dad might not be there at midnight, when you have to decide whether or not to invite your date to your apartment for "a cup of coffee." But soon you'll find you won't just be doing the wrong thing on your date, you'll be lying about how you spent the weekend.

Whether or not Paul was there, the Philippians toed the line morally. Perhaps they understood that they weren't obeying Paul, but God. Paul wasn't being a rule maker. He showed them the best way to have a terrific relationship with God. They wanted that, so they followed the "rules."

Father God, sometimes Your ways seem so restrictive. I need to remember they're leading me to a happier, more holy life.

December 14

Why do you boast of evil, you mighty man?
Why do you boast all day long,
you who are a disgrace in the eyes of God?
PSALM 52:1

You're working hard, trying to be honest, even though you don't get a large salary and could really use a few things. Then a coworker boasts about a killing he made by doing wrong to someone else.

Why him and not me? you may wonder.

Don't follow him. First, chances are you can't duplicate what he's done. You're likely to get caught if you try to repeat the same slick deal.

But even if you could repeat his method and no one caught you, it wouldn't be worth the price. When you decided to pray, you'd feel disgrace taking up space between you and God. You'd wonder if He was listening very closely. Should you escape that quiet time without confessing the sin, you'd start feeling uncomfortable, so you'd pray less often.

Soon you wouldn't pray at all, and your church attendance would start slipping.

Don't listen to those who boast of evil; instead do some of your own boasting in the God who saved you.

Turn me back from sin, Lord. Close my ears to sinners' boasting.

December 15

The Sovereign LORD will wipe away
the tears from all faces.
ISAIAH 25:8

I just wish Christmas were over," Marta insisted. "All those bright lights just make me sadder this year."

About a month before Christmas, Marta's grandmother had died, and it hurt to remember how every other year, a few days before Christmas, they'd baked cookies together and sung carols at the piano. Marta wasn't in a holiday mood.

Tinsel and lights didn't shine brightly for Marta that Christmas, but something else did—Jesus. Whenever sadness tried to overwhelm her, she turned to Him in prayer. Though nothing could remove her loss, Marta felt Jesus reminding her that Christmas wasn't just tinsel and lights. It was the kind of love Christians like her grandmother could share because they believed in a baby born in Bethlehem.

Is the holy Child your bright light this year?

Thank You, Lord, that we can enjoy the bright lights of Christmas. But I'm glad they just symbolize the light You give.

December 16

Now faith is being sure of what
we hope for and certain of what
we do not see.
HEBREWS 11:1

Am I crazy to believe in this? Has that thought ever run through your mind when you were thinking about the Virgin Birth, Moses and the burning bush, or the Resurrection?

Logically, these events don't seem to make much sense. After all, each was a one-time incident that no one can re-create. Many question the truth of these biblical accounts.

In some circles, people have become so doubtful that they try to explain away these phenomena. But such would-be Christians have missed the point, haven't they? Of course none of these events can be explained. It's a matter of faith, not intellectual "sight."

As we exercise our faith, even though we can't work out exactly how such things happened, we can begin to see how it's all part of God's plan.

Then we're believing in Jesus.

Lord, I praise You for being so marvelous and powerful that You boggle my mind. Help me trust in Your power. I want to walk by faith.

December 17

*Now therefore hearken, O Israel,
unto the statutes and unto the judgments,
which I teach you, for to do them, that ye may
live, and go in and possess the land which the
Lord God of your fathers giveth you.*
DEUTERONOMY 4:1, KJV

Do you avoid obeying God's Word and only approach Him when you need something?

If so, you probably struggle in your Christian walk. Seeing God as a sort of "celestial Santa Claus" shows a selfishness that separates you from God's blessing.

The nation of Israel followed God when it was convenient. They got a blessing—the Promised Land—but only on a forty-year revised schedule.

Obey God because you love Him and want to be more like Him, and He gives you your Promised Land immediately, not forty years late. His blessings are real, but not automatic.

God's giving isn't tit for tat—it's all-out sharing from a Father who loves children who listen to Him. But He can't reward disobedient children.

So listen to your Father.

Father, I know You want to bless me. Keep me from sin that ruins blessing.

December 18

*Let God weigh me in honest scales
and he will know that I am blameless.*
JOB 31:6

Job seemed to have everything—a happy family, lots of money, and a great relationship with God. Who wouldn't envy him?

Until disaster struck.

Suddenly Job was scratching his sores, sitting atop a dunghill, without a supportive family—and with friends like *his,* no one needed an enemy! Where had Job gone wrong? Hadn't he been honest with everyone he'd dealt with? He hadn't made his millions by walking over others. This honest man cried out to God.

But God didn't seem to answer.

We know. We try our best at work, but we get laid off. We're honest with our money, but someone else takes our girl to a play, while we go to the park. We pray, but nothing changes.

Has God forgotten us? No way! The answer may not come overnight—it didn't for Job. But in the end, blessing overwhelmed him. God does that for us, too. Sometimes the more time He takes to develop a blessing, the better it is.

When Your blessings come slowly, keep me patient, Lord.

December 19

A man will. . .be united to his wife,
and they will become one flesh.
GENESIS 2:24

"And they lived happily ever after." Deep down inside, every couple would like this tribute to apply to their marriage. Even if you're still single, you probably imagine yourself finding Mr. or Ms. Right.

No one gets married to experience the pain of divorce. But about half of American marriages end that way. So you may ask, *Can I be sure it'll work for me?*

Marital guarantees don't exist. You can't know that hard times will never hit you—everyone has them. But a marriage God puts together can be even better than the "happily ever after" variety, because in a God-made marriage, happiness doesn't depend on circumstances.

Real marital unity comes when two people count on the commitment they made before God and trust Him to pull them through any problem. It's amazing what they can experience and still stay together. Their happiness in each other comes from God, not their own power. So the more they turn to Him, the stronger their marriage grows.

You can have a God-made marriage. Just ask Him for one and wait for His timing.

Thank You, Lord, that You, not a storyteller, put marriages together.

December 20

*Therefore let us stop
passing judgment on one another.*
ROMANS 14:13

"If I have to listen to 'Jingle Bell Rock' one more time, I think I'll scream!" Carrie complained to her brother. "It's not that I don't love Mom or want to spend time with her before the holidays, but I can't stand that tape! You'd think, as a Christian, she'd listen to something *spiritual*."

"I know," Ted agreed. "And if you try to play another tape—!"

Is the Christmas rush making you tense and irritable? Has anger billowed in while joy's evaporated from your holiday? When the shopping, gift wrapping, and "pleasures" of Christmas become a strain, maybe it's time to look at what you're celebrating.

It's not how much you can cram into a holiday season, how you can celebrate "properly," or how many last-minute gifts you need to shop for. Even if you couldn't dress the house with fancy decorations or buy any gifts, you could still celebrate Christmas. After all, Jesus didn't come to create a holiday season, He came to touch people's hearts with God's love.

Help others to see Jesus, and you *will* have a blessed Christmas.

Lord Jesus, whatever else I do this Christmas, help me reach out with Your love.

December 21

Thou shalt neither vex a stranger, nor oppress him: for ye were strangers in the land of Egypt.
EXODUS 22:21, KJV

You move to a new town or a new school, and for the first few days you feel really strange. You don't know where to go for anything you need. You don't know who to ask for advice.

Then someone comes along and tells you about some good stores, the best bank, and maybe a great doctor. All of a sudden you're beginning to find your feet. You feel more secure, and life balances out again.

God knows what it feels like to be in a strange place (after all, didn't Jesus leave His home to come to earth?). He understands that sometimes you have to go to a new place (didn't he call Abram to move?).

Maybe because of that, He tells us to have compassion for the new person on the block. We don't need to wonder if we should stretch out a welcoming hand. God's been there before us, greeting the outcast.

Thank You, Lord, for caring for me when I'm in a new place. Help me to reach out to others who are feeling strange in a new town, a new job, or a new country.

December 22

A man's wisdom gives him patience;
it is to his glory to overlook an offense.
PROVERBS 19:11

Ever gotten stuck at an airport? Maybe your flight gets canceled—or you drive in to pick up a family member or friend and see *delayed* in place of an arrival time.

Either way, you're stuck. The only decision you really can make is how you'll handle the situation. Will you gripe and complain until everyone within a ten-foot radius decides to "get something to eat"? Or will you make use of your time by catching up on reading, praying, or making a new friend of a fellow traveler?

We can't always control life, but we can take charge of our reaction to it. Gripers don't enjoy those hours of their lives, but those who learn a new skill, draw closer to God, or share life with someone new can feel blessed.

Though self-control doesn't always come easy to me, Lord, I know it's part of the fruit of Your Spirit. When I have to wait, help me to bear a good crop for you.

December 23

There are articles not only of gold and silver,
but also of wood and clay;
some are for noble purposes
and some for ignoble.
If a man cleanses himself from the latter,
he will be an instrument for noble purposes.
2 TIMOTHY 2:20–21

When you set your Christmas table, you use your nicest tablecloth, your best dinnerware and silver.

If guests came and found a burlap cloth on the table, topped with cheap plastic dishes, they'd wonder if money was tight for you. Next year you might receive a better tablecloth or dishes.

If that's all you have, no one can wave a wand and improve that tableware. The plastic will always be plastic, and the burlap cloth will never be linen. They are what they are.

Some Christians, Paul says, are fine silver bowls —others are cheap plastic ones. But this plastic can change. Believers who cleanse themselves from sin become more like Jesus, and like silver bowls, people begin to see His reflection in them. Spiritually, plastic turns to silver.

Are you sitting inside the closet on the best days of the year? Or can Jesus use you for His celebrations? He'd like to show you off on His holiday table.

Lord Jesus, on this holiday, help me shine for You.

December 24

*She will give birth to a son,
and you are to give him the name Jesus,
because he will save his people from their sins.*
MATTHEW 1:21

If Santa Claus can't deliver all his gifts, Christmas can't come," a children's story tells you. As a Christian, you know that really isn't true, don't you?

Enjoy giving and receiving gifts this year, and be generous, but don't lose sight of the real Gift this season. Even if "Santa" didn't come—if all your family and friends forgot to get you gifts or couldn't deliver them by December 25—you'd still have a wonderful present.

It wouldn't be a nicely wrapped package under the tree, but the nicest package couldn't compete with it. It would last longer than a CD, sweatshirt, or computer.

Imagine not feeling as if you made the *wrong* decision and forever paid the consequences. Think of feeling *really* free to do what was right.

That's God's gift to you this season. Christmas came in the person of Jesus, who frees you from sin.

All you have to do is trust in Him.

Lord Jesus, You are the best Christmas gift available. I need to trust in Your forgiveness every day.

December 25

*For unto you is born this day in the city of
David a Saviour, which is Christ the Lord.*
LUKE 2:11, KJV

What an unusual night that was for a ragged
bunch of shepherds huddled out in the cold! After
being nearly scared to death by an angel reflecting
God's splendor, they heard the wonderful Good
News that God had fulfilled His promise. Then
they, of all people, were invited to witness what
God had done.

The shepherds could hardly wait to go to Bethlehem. Imagine! Through the ages Hebrews had
waited for this and, unworthy as they were, *their*
eyes were about to see the Messiah!

They hurried off, not to see a king in his might,
but a peasant baby in a common stable—a person
much like them. Respected religious leaders probably would have sneered at such an unlikely Redeemer. But the humble shepherds trusted in the
One God showed them that night, and His light
filled their lives.

Are you overflowing with the Savior's light?
Ask God to forgive your sins and let Him take
charge of your life, and the true meaning of Christmas will flood your soul, too.

*Jesus, I want Your light to fill every part of my
being. During this special season, let me show
others the light You bring.*

December 26

For the Lord himself will come down
from heaven, with a loud command,
with the voice of the archangel
and with the trumpet call of God,
and the dead in Christ will rise first.
1 THESSALONIANS 4:16

Remember your childhood anticipation of Christmas? You could barely wait until the day came and carefully counted the days, then the hours, until you could open the presents stacked under the tree.

As a Christian, you have another, even more exciting day to look forward to. Though you don't know when it's coming, you can be as sure of it as you are of Christmas Day. It's the day the Babe returns as Savior, in all His glory.

Though the world could overlook Jesus the first time, at His Second Coming every eye will be unable to ignore Him. Doubts will be shed when the world sees His glory.

Can you wait to unwrap all the glories God wants to share with you? It could be just another day or hour or moment away.

What a wonderful day, Lord, when I'll see You face-to-face. Though I feel as if I just can't wait, let me use this time to draw others to You.

December 27

Man looks at the outward appearance,
but the LORD looks at the heart.
1 SAMUEL 16:7

Josh can't be a Christian!" Sheila exclaimed. "He may come to church, but he just sits in the pew. Have you ever known him to take part in anything but Sunday mornings or help out in any way? And look at those friends he brings to church—each one looks as if he'd be more at home at a biker's convention than here!"

Too bad Sheila couldn't see into Josh's heart. Her judgments couldn't have been more wrong. In some areas Josh got a slow start as a Christian, but his warm heart for bikers led him to reach out to people the church rarely touched. A few years later, his ministry to these people bore much fruit.

Thank God that He sees beyond our brothers' and sisters' criticisms and into our hearts. Sin can't hide our real value or keep Him from lifting us out of its mire.

Are you plopped in mire today or reaching out to God?

Thank You, Lord, for seeing my heart, not just my actions. Make me clean from the inside out.

December 28

*"For God so loved the world that
he gave his one and only Son,
that whoever believes in him shall not perish
but have eternal life."*
JOHN 3:16

Eternal life"—have you ever thought of time without end, stretching on and on? But not dull, useless hours or overly hectic days—time for God's kind of life that's continually fresh and exciting without being rushed.

Most of us can rattle off John 3:16 without even thinking about it. But have we thought about what we'll do with endless life with the Creator of the universe?

If we listed everything we'd like to do in heaven, most of us would have trouble filling up a month, much less eternity. From an earthly point of view, we can imagine boredom setting in early.

But living in the home of "new life" leaves no room for boredom. Scripture only gives us faint glimpses, but certainly a Father who took such efforts to save us wouldn't skimp on our shared eternity.

No matter what we do in heaven, God will be bigger than our wildest dreams.

Lord, when I think of time without limits, my mind goes fuzzy. I only know I want to glorify You with every atom of my being.

December 29

For that ye ought to say, If the Lord will,
we shall live, and do this, or that.
JAMES 4:15, KJV

What does James mean in this verse?" Kirsten asked. "Sounds as if he's saying we should never make plans. If I did that, my life'd be a mess!"

Her Bible study leader explained that God wasn't frowning on our making plans. But He doesn't want us to get caught up in our plans and never look to Him for guidance. Planning done without God leads down a dead-end street.

As the end of the year nears, you're looking forward to 365 new days filled with career and personal opportunities. Maybe lots of options vie for your attention: Should you move in with friends, take a job in another state, or start dating someone new?

Though you see the exciting changes ahead, you don't have a God's-eye view of your life. He sees the big picture and wants to help you make the right choices.

So why not ask Him what the next step is?

This new year needs to be filled, Lord. Let it overflow with Your will for me.

December 30

The evil deeds of a wicked man ensnare him;
the cords of his sin hold him fast.
He will die for lack of discipline,
led astray by his own great folly.
PROVERBS 5:22–23

Tie a puppy out on a leash, and you're bound to come back a few minutes later and find her all wrapped up in her own cord. Though she didn't mean to get in trouble, she is, and she can't untie herself to get free.

That's the way sin wraps people up. They're playing at life, doing all the things they enjoy and taking no heed of the way they're getting tied up in wrongdoing. Once they're held fast, the only one who can free them is God.

Even once you know Him, it takes discipline to avoid getting tied up in sin. Instead of foolishly walking down a road of ease, keep an eye on where you're heading. Maybe you need to make some lifestyle changes.

Don't scratch every party off your schedule, but balance your free time by helping out at church, doing a favor for a neighbor, or spending time in serious Bible study. Make your free time count for Christ.

Every moment of my life is Yours, Jesus. Help me make each one count for You.

December 31

Forgetting what is behind
and straining toward what is ahead,
I press on toward the goal to win the prize
for which God has called me
heavenward in Christ Jesus.
PHILIPPIANS 3:13–14

You've made it through another year! Look back, and you can see some things you wish you hadn't done—and some good things you never found time for. Maybe you made a career choice that's not so great, or you had some wonderful friends with whom you lost touch.

Don't wallow in your past mistakes—jump beyond them. There are few things in life that you can't change, if you're willing to spend time and effort on them.

Sure, rewriting your resume and contacting companies isn't your favorite free-time project. But your new job might be worth it. Calling a friend might be hard to fit into your schedule—and you might get his answering machine a few times—but imagine rekindling the faith you shared last summer!

Paul knew that moving ahead spiritually meant forgetting past mistakes and moving on. You can do that!

Lord, a new year gives me a chance to look back—
or leap forward. Help me move ahead in faith.

Index

Mistakes

Jan. 21, Jan. 26, Feb. 18, Apr. 19, May 4,
Jul. 20, Aug. 21, Nov. 15, Dec. 7, Dec. 31

Money

Jan. 2, Jan. 3, Jan. 11, Jan. 20, Jan. 27, Feb. 6,
Feb. 8, Feb. 13, Mar. 4, Mar. 27, Apr. 15,
Apr. 28, Jul. 18, Jul. 19, Nov. 28

O

"Older" people

Jan. 12, Jan. 17, Jun. 2

P

Parents

Jan. 11, Jan. 13, Jan. 29, Mar. 1, May 9,
May 18, May 20, Jun. 30, Jul. 22, Nov. 17

Planning

Jan. 3, Jan. 18, Feb. 7, Apr. 11, May 10,
Jun. 26, Jul. 6, Jul. 24, Aug. 3, Aug. 13,
Sep. 2, Sep. 12, Nov. 4, Dec. 3, Dec. 29

Pride

Apr. 30, Jun. 27, Aug. 16, Aug. 27, Dec. 7

Principles

Jan. 5, Feb. 9, Jul. 4

Promises

Jan. 7, Jan. 26, Mar. 10, Mar. 24, Apr. 16,
May 26, Jun. 22, Jul. 31, Aug. 6, Sep. 16,
Sep. 17

T

V

W